THE POET AS PHILOSOPHER

The author and Yale University Press gratefully acknowledge the generous assistance of the Center for Medieval and Renaissance Studies, University of California, Los Angeles, in the preparation of the manuscript.

the poet as philosopher

PETRARCH AND
THE FORMATION OF
RENAISSANCE CONSCIOUSNESS

CHARLES TRINKAUS

Yale University Press   1979   New Haven and London

Published with assistance from Horace H. Rackham School of Graduate Studies, The University of Michigan.

Set in IBM Press Roman type.
Printed in the United States of America by Vail-Ballou Press, Binghamton, N.Y.

Published in Great Britain, Europe, Africa, and Asia (except Japan) by Yale University Press, Ltd., London. Distributed in Australia and New Zealand by Book & Film Services, Artarmon, N.S.W., Australia; and in Japan by Harper & Row, Publishers, Tokyo Office.

Library of Congress Cataloging in Publication Data

Trinkaus, Charles Edward, 1911–
   The poet as philosopher.

   Bibliography: p.
   Includes index.
   1. Petrarca, Francesco, 1304–1374–Philosophy–
Addresses, essays, lectures. 2. Petrarca, Francesco,
1304–1374–Criticism and interpretation–Addresses,
essays, lectures. I. Title.
PQ4542.T7   851'.1   79–64069
ISBN 0-300-02327-8

For Pauline

Contents

Preface

The historical and artistic importance of Francesco Petrarca (July 20, 1304–July 19, 1374) is witnessed by the
continuing stream of scholarly and popular studies of his
life and poetry. It is no accident that he has had a central
place in my own search for the nature and motivations of
Renaissance humanism since my dissertation studies some
forty years ago. Having dealt with him as a major figure of
humanist religious thought in *In Our Image and Likeness*
(1970), it had not been my intention to write further on
Petrarch. But the six-hundredth anniversary of the poet's
death in 1974 prompted invitations to lecture at the World
Petrarch Congress of the Folger Library, at the Dante
Society of Toronto, and at the Society for the Humanities
of Cornell University. A fourth lecture was prepared for
The University of Michigan's Boccaccio Festival. These
lectures were written sequentially with the specific theme
of Petrarch and philosophy in mind. They have therefore
been converted with some revisions into chapters 1, 2, 4,
and 5, respectively, of this book. Chapter 3 is an exten-
sively reworked version of an essay first written over thirty
years ago and published in 1954 in volume II of *Osiris*,
dedicated to Lynn Thorndike.

I wish to thank the sponsors of these congresses and
lecture series for the opportunity to extend my thoughts
about Petrarch, and the directors of Uitgerverij "De Tem-
pel" (Bruges, Belgium), publishers of *Osiris*, for permission
to use material from my earlier essay. Part of the work
was carried out during my tenure of fellowships from the

National Endowment for the Humanities and the John
Simon Guggenheim Foundation, and I am very grateful
for their support. My largest and most grateful debt is to
Professor Fredi Chiappelli, Director of the U.C.L.A. Center for Medieval and Renaissance Studies, and to his staff,
for providing the many apt and helpful suggestions that
have enormously improved the manuscript. I wish, finally,
to thank The University of Michigan's Horace H. Rackham School of Graduate Studies for its financial support
of this publication.

As the title of this volume suggests, I do not believe that
Petrarch's work and career as a poet should be thought of
and studied separately from his role as a humanist. And
yet the bifurcation between his Italian *Canzoniere* and his
Latin prose works, together with the sad isolation of literature and history departments (not to mention philosophy,
which too often disdains the past in all its aspects), has
traditionally imposed such a division. My own contribution, because I have been totally trained in the one and am
totally a tyro in the other, necessarily continues what I
deplore. I only hope to be able to suggest some ways in
which Petrarch's poetic mentality penetrated and shaped
his thought. Our finest literary scholars have always had to
do the reverse with his lyrics. Much will also be said about
rhetoric, which is becoming a familiar story to students of
the Renaissance. But rhetoric, although in my view a *ter-
tium quid*, was also grasped by Petrarch within the terms
of his activity as a poet. Hence he was truly a *vates* whose
historical role was prophetic.

The reader may follow my expositions and interpreta-
tions of Petrarch's moral philosophy in the chapters themselves. I dealt with his religious thought in *In Our Image
and Likeness*, and although the themes developed in this
present work are closely related and overlap in places, I
have tried not to repeat either the material or the ideas

except where it was essential to the argument. I have not examined in any extended way—although with Petrarch all such distinctions are unreal—Petrarch's contribution to the development of Renaissance culture in the areas of philology and of historical consciousness. For this I should mention, in the great sea of significant contributions, the classic articles of Giuseppe Billanovich, Theodor E. Mommsen, and Thomas M. Greene.[1]

1. Giuseppe Billanovich, "Petrarch and the Textual Tradition of Livy," *Journal of the Warburg and Courtauld Institutes* 14 (1951); Theodor E. Mommsen, "Petrarch's Conception of the Dark Ages," in *Medieval and Renaissance Studies*, ed. E. F. Rice, Jr. (Ithaca, 1959); Thomas M. Greene, "Petrarch and the Humanist Hermeneutic," in *Italian Literature, Roots and Branches: Essays in Honor of Thomas Goddard Bergin*, ed. G. Rimanelli and K. J. Atchity (New Haven, 1976).

1

Petrarch and Classical Philosophy

Petrarch's knowledge of ancient thought was amazingly extensive. Yet how he incorporated this knowledge into his own philosophy is not entirely clear. De Nolhac and Sabbadini laid the foundations for our efforts to reconstruct Petrarch's classical humanism, and Billanovich, Pellegrin, and Wilkins, with major assistance from such scholars of the previous generation as Rossi and Bosco, have come close to completing the edifice.[1] But scholars continue to differ on the questions of what ideas Petrarch drew from his knowledge of ancient philosophies, and how, to what degree, and when he made use of his readings.[2]

Petrarch identified himself at various times as a poet, a historian, a rhetorician, and a moral philosopher.[3] His awareness of the classical philosophical heritage was formed by his responses to it in all of these roles. Yet the way in which his conception of ancient philosophy was shaped by his sensibilities as a poet is of special interest. It

1. I refer here to the names of some of the greatest Petrarch scholars. For full references to the works of these authors, see List of Works Cited. To the names of Nolhac, Sabbadini, Rossi, Bosco, Billanovich, Pellegrin, and Wilkins, there should certainly be added Guido Martellotti and B. L. Ullman. See under "Petrarca" and "Studies."

2. Cf. the following, which concern Petrarch's "inconsistencies": Klaus Heitmann, "Augustins Lehre," "L'insegnamento agostiniano," and Fortuna und Virtus; Hans Baron, "The Evolution of Petrarch's Thought," "Petrarch's Secretum," and "Petrarch: His Inner Struggles"; Jerrold E. Seigel, Rhetoric and Philosophy, chap. 2, "Ideals of Eloquence and Silence in Petrarch." I have tried to resolve some of the dilemmas in "Petrarch: Man between Despair and Grace," chap. 1 of Image.

3. Cf. P. O. Kristeller, "Il Petrarca, l'umanesimo e la scolastica."

is likely that Petrarch understood classical philosophy better through Vergil and Horace than through the philosophers he came to know, which suggests that his grasp of ancient philosophy was more characteristically that of a poet than that of a historian. It also suggests that it was possibly through the medium of his poetic understanding of ancient thought that he was incited to conceive and fulfill the roles of both rhetorician and moral philosopher.

Petrarch's kind of poetry had a special relationship to the new mode of philosophical consciousness that was emerging in the Renaissance to which he made so important a contribution. Aristotle, in explaining his famous claim that poetry is more philosophical than history, said that the philosophical character of poetry may be seen in the universal nature of its statements, "whereas those of history are singulars."[4] We must recognize the universality of Petrarch's poetry. Yet we must recognize its subjectivity as well. His use of emotional experience, the recreation in emotion of that experience, and the imagined prolongation and projection of it in the *Canzoniere* underline the difference between his poetry and the kind Aristotle discussed. It is not enough to say that Petrarch's verse was lyric, and hence more personal, whereas Aristotle was referring to epic and dramatic, and thus more objectified poetry. Petrarch's great achievement was that he realized poetic objectivity through the medium of subjective experience.

To say that Petrarch thought philosophically as a poet is not to minimize his importance as a philosopher but to point out his unique mode of thinking. Petrarch's work, whether poetic, historical, or philosophical, is of critical importance as the first major manifestation of the great transformation from the objective mode of classical

---

4. *Poetica*, 1451a–b. (Bywater trans.)

thought and perception to the subjective Renaissance and modern modes.[5] While many questions remain concerning the character and the extent of such a shift in the basic conceptions of Western art and thought, Petrarch gave a powerful impulse to the movement toward subjectivity.

Under this large assumption about the differences in basic patterns of thought and perception in the ancient and modern worlds, Petrarch's manifold contradictions seem to fall neatly into place. But it is far too neat. It is like saying that we are all romantics in our modern retrospective classicism, since we regard antiquity through the screen of our own affections and imaginations, imitating it and idealizing it because of our own needs and motivations. We view it as at once distant and highly relevant, a historical perspective that Petrarch helped to shape. This insight, stressed by Panofsky, is true in a sense, but it threatens to dissolve amidst our own subjectivity. Not all of modern thought and perception is subjective; otherwise we could not make claims to science or to scholarly understanding. Even Petrarch helped develop the "objective" study of antiquity. On the other hand, not all ancient thought and perception was substantive and objectivistic. Important aspects of it, and especially much of what attracted Petrarch, pointed the way toward more modern modalities.[6]

5. More than twenty years ago, Leo Spitzer showed how the Latin verse of Pontano and Poliziano broke out of the mold of antiquity, unable to dispel the personal lyric quality so freely evident in their Italian poems, despite their classicizing aims and conscious imitations. See his "Latin Renaissance Poetry." Edward Cranz has more recently stressed a similar transformation of the philosophical perceptions of antiquity and early Christianity in the High and late Middle Ages, and specifically in Petrarch; see "Cusanus" and "1100 A.D." Professor Cranz is currently preparing a major study of this theme which is briefly summarized in these papers.

6. A good antidote to the objectivistic stereotype of the classical mentality is the comprehensive survey of Rodolfo Mondolfo, *La Comprensione del*

Petrarch's attitudes toward the philosophies of his own day will be discussed more fully in chapters 3, 4, and 5. Essentially, however, his inclination was to value philosophy primarily for its contribution to the strengthening of human virtue. The tendency of contemporary scholasticism was to regard discussions of substantive questions in theology as of limited viability and, almost by default, to move toward the exegetical and pastoral. Petrarch expressed great suspicion regarding both the emphasis on dialectical analysis and the interest in Aristotelian natural philosophy of his contemporaries. He seems, however, to have had a rather scanty knowledge of medieval philosophy. He was certainly not very sympathetic to the possibility that the vogue for dialectic in fourteenth-century scholastic thought might have represented a parallel development to his desire to consider philosophical thought as humanly centered and motivated.[7] Petrarch also seems not to have been aware of those fourteenth-century contributions to natural philosophy that represented experimental departures, however limited, from an all-determining Aristotelian physical framework. It is Petrarch's knowledge of ancient philosophy, however, that is my main concern here.

The philosophical thought of the ancient Greeks and Romans is an enormous, highly diverse body of material. It is now known only through those texts that survived in

---

soggetto. For Petrarch's contribution to the scholarly study of antiquity, see Billanovich, "Petrarch and the Textual Tradition of Livy," and Roberto Weiss, *Renaissance Discovery,* 30–38. For Panofsky's thesis concerning the Renaissance view of antiquity, see *Renaissance and Renascences,* 108–13 and passim.

7. The use of dialectic seems to have been resorted to by many thinkers to compensate for their loss of confidence in the reliability of metaphysical speculation. They, as the humanists after them, sought to make precise statements about the relationship of thought to perception and language rather than sweeping assertions about what, in their view, could be known only vaguely.

medieval manuscripts or have been recovered from papyri in the past century. These texts are supplemented by descriptive accounts by other ancient authors and modern collections of scattered quotations from ancient, early Christian, Syriac, Arabic, Jewish, and Byzantine writers. It is tempting to make use of modern scholarship and historical sophistication to give a single characterization to this diverse mass (as Cranz has so suggestively done; see note 5). But this is clearly a risky undertaking. Some portions of ancient philosophy are rather well known, possibly even understood by modern historians and philosophers. But others, even when reported to be of the greatest importance in antiquity, are unknown, or hardly known. A further element of complication is that ancient philosophical writings contain much that is religious, magical, scientific, literary, critical, and rhetorical, while ancient writings in these other disciplines also contain much that is philosophical.

Ancient philosophy as it is presently known includes the partially understood pre-Socratic speculators concerned with the cosmos and the "nature" of things—the *physici*. Also identified are the equally poorly understood teachers of political discourse whom we call, by their own designation, the *sophistes*. Some Sophists claimed inspiration from contemporary Greek tragedy and traced their ancestry through the poetic tradition back as far as Homer and Hesiod. They were not only admirers of tragedy; their ideas are reflected in Euripides and mocked in Aristophanes. The *physici* preceded and were contemporary with the Sophists, some of whom had studied under and been influenced by them. The *physici*, conventionally divided into Ionians and Eleatics, seem to have followed our loose distinction between empiricists and metaphysicians, though this seems to dissolve in almost every instance thought to be adequately understood. The Sophists seem to have drawn from both the empirical and metaphysical traditions of the pre-Socratics.

Petrarch, of course, knew far less about either the *physici* or the Sophists than do modern scholars. For the most part, he scattered references through his works and his correspondence to sayings or anecdotes of an early Greek or other ancient thinker which helped to reinforce or exemplify his point rhetorically. Of the pre-Socratics, [Petrarch devotes greatest attention to Pythagoras and Heraclitus. Pythagoras he knows only as a sage, moral reformer, and orator, but he cites him frequently because of his great reputation for wisdom in the later ancient sources with which Petrarch was familiar.[8] He knows something of Heraclitus's ideas from Seneca and therefore as the Stoics had interpreted him for their own purposes, but he used these ideas more substantively. He cites Heraclitus twice to assert the chaotic and fluctuating character of the world of human experience under the domination of fortune, once at the beginning of book 2 of the *De remediis* and again at the beginning of book 2 of his *De otio religioso*.[9] Valerius Maximus's *Factorum et dictorum memorabilium libri* was a major source for the anecdotes and sayings of others. The writings of Cicero, Seneca, Aulus Gellius, and Macrobius also served him well.

Petrarch hardly seems to have known of the Sophists except as enemies of Socrates and Plato, mentioning Gorgias's great age[10] and quoting Protagoras as Pythagoras (though significantly).[11] The name "Sophist" he reserves for the scholastic dialecticians and natural philosophers of

8. He scatters twelve references to anecdotes and sayings through *Le familiari*. There are two entries on Pythagoras in his *Rer. mem.*; they closely follow Justin, *Epitome*; Cicero, *Tusc.* 5. 3–4, and *De inven.* 2. 1.

9. Cf. *Image*, 49, 195–96, 343 nn. 103–05, 400 n. 38; *De rem.* in *Op. om.*, 121–25; *De otio*, 59–60. Cf. Seneca, *Epist.*, 58. 23.

10. *Rer. fam.*, 6. 3. 17.

11. Nachod, 125. Cf. *Image*, 50.

his day, the twisters of truth and vendors of learning. Socrates was admired by the humanists principally for the emphasis he placed on man and for his self-knowledge, education, and morality. The modern dispute about whether Socrates must also be seen as a Sophist or as Plato portrays him, their archenemy, had little meaning for the Renaissance humanists.[12]

Petrarch, however, is surprisingly uninterested in Socrates, even considering the paucity of his available knowledge. With all his yearning to know Plato, he seems to have seriously studied only the Calcidius partial translation of the *Timaeus*, though he also possessed a copy of the Henricus Aristippus translation of the *Phaedo* (BN. lat. 6567A).[13] For his scattered anecdotal references to Socrates, Petrarch resorts to Valerius Maximus, Cicero, and Apuleius's *De deo Socratis*, slender pickings to be sure. There is little expression in Petrarch of the strenuous admiration that Salutati and other humanists showed for Socrates. The crucial and much quoted statement from

12. Ancient historians have recently given greater recognition to the Sophists. They are frequently designated as the founders of ancient humanism or of the humanist tradition. Whether the rather scanty knowledge of and interest in the Sophists on the part of Renaissance humanists can be accounted for is not of present concern. But there is no doubt that the humanists followed Cicero in considering Socrates as the true founder of their own tradition. What they would have thought of the Sophists if they had possessed or known of Cicero's lost translation of Plato's *Protagoras* cannot be said. See Werner Jaeger, *Paideia*, vol. 1, book 2, chap. 3, "The Sophists"; W. K. C. Guthrie, *Greek Philosophy*, vol. 3, part 1, "The World of the Sophists"; Mario Untersteiner, *The Sophists*. On Renaissance humanists and the Sophists, see my "Protagoras in the Renaissance."

13. Pellegrin, *La bibliothèque*, 105, lists no. 148 of the 1426 inventory of the Visconti-Sforza Library (*Phedon Platonis*) as Paris, BN. lat. 6567A. Cf. L. Minio-Paluello, "Il Fedone latino," 107–13. De Nolhac, *Pétrarque et l'humanisme*, 2, 141 and n. 3, expresses surprise that Petrarch had not made greater use of the *Phaedo*. But see L. Minio-Paluello on Petrarch's marginalia to BN. lat. 6567A. He suggests (113) that Petrarch may have read this work only in his final years.

Cicero's *Tusculan Disputations*[14]—"But Socrates was the first who brought down philosophy from the heavens and, snatched from the stars, forced it to live on earth among men and to deal with morals and the affairs of men"—was curiously cited in a letter to Gerardo as an example of how philosophers ridiculed each other. He refers to Aristotle's ridicule, cited in Cicero's *De officiis*,[15] of Isocrates (misreading the name as "Socrates") for his mercenary behavior.

It might seem that Petrarch's affirmations of the importance of moral philosophy would have made him more responsive to Socrates. His admiration of Cicero would seemingly have led him to note Cicero's addition to the passage just cited from the *Tusculans*: "I have principally adhered to that (sect) which, in my opinion, Socrates himself followed: and argue so as to conceal my own opinions, while I deliver others from their errors, and so discover what has the greatest appearance of probability in every question. . ." Petrarch only rarely refers to the passage in the *Academica*[16] where Socrates is asserted to have been the first to discuss moral philosophy and to have affirmed "nothing himself but to refute others, to assert that he knows nothing except the fact of his own ignorance." Toward the end of *On His Own Ignorance* he does cite Socrates' "This one thing I know, that I know nothing," and adds to it Arcesilas's saying that "even this knowing nothing cannot be known" (both passages are apparently drawn from the *Academica*), but his purpose is to reject or ridicule this attitude along with a general condemnation of philosophy. "A glorious philosophy, this, that either confesses ignorance or precludes even the knowledge of this ignorance."[17]

14. *Tusc.*, 5.4.
15. *Rer. fam.*, 10.5.15; *De offic.*, 1.1.
16. *Acad.*, 1.4.15.
17. *De ignor.*, Nachod, 126.

Nonetheless the general influence of Socrates on this work cannot be excluded. Though different in tone and method from the *Dialogues*, Petrarch built it around the ironic stance of his own acknowledged ignorance and the unacknowledged ignorance of many others. This stance he might well have borrowed from Socrates. He at least understood the rhetorical impact of this posture, although he had not been able to read Plato's *Apology* and did not indicate his Socratic model. Yet he used this ploy to draw conclusions similar to those that Plato perhaps intended for Socrates' defense. It is one of several examples where Petrarch employs classical models in order to assert or discover his own cultural identity through an act of role playing.

Petrarch wrote four comments on Socrates in his *Rerum memorandarum libri* which show him to have been aware early in his philosophical career of the chief anecdotes about Socrates and his reputation. Under the rubric "On Leisure and Solitude"[18] he briefly cites the anecdote from Cicero's *De senectute*[19] about Socrates as an old man learning to play the lyre. In the next rubric, "On Study and Learning," he repeats the topos of Socrates having brought learning down to earth and turned it from the dimensions of the heavens to the interior of the human heart. "Beginning to treat of the diseases and motions of the soul and of their remedies and the virtues, he was the *primus artifex* of moral philosophy, and as Valerius said, *'vite magister optimus'*."[20] Skipping the third, his fourth item under "On Oracles" is equally brief. He narrates from Cicero's *De divinatione* Socrates' advice to Xenophon to join the expedition of Cyrus and his adjunct that this was a human counsel and that in the case of more obscure matters he

18. *Rer. mem.*, 1.9. (Unless lines and pages are specified, numbers refer to book and section.)
19. *De sen.*, 8.26.
20. *Rer. mem.*, 1.27.

should consult the oracle. However, Petrarch misread "Epicurus" for Cyrus and proceeded to berate Socrates for being an Epicurean. "But how much better you were and of how much sounder counsel than he to whom you sent your disciple, except in this one matter that he seemed to you the best and most advisable [leader]."[21] Apart from the extraordinary anachronism, one may wonder how Socrates could possibly have seemed an influence in the direction of Epicurus to Petrarch.

His major discussion of Socrates in the *Rerum memorandarum libri* was under "On Wisdom," cataloguing sayings of the wise. Though it may not eliminate a suspicion that Petrarch was somewhat lukewarm in his admiration of Socrates because of his seeming scepticism, Petrarch lays forth his amplification of Valerius Maximus's essentially moralistic and Stoic version. He starts with the Socratic advice to seek nothing from the gods except what truly benefits us and expands the sparse treatment of this theme by his source into a favorite review of all the evils of a Christian's false desires. But he uses as his model not Socrates but the tenth *Satire* of Juvenal.[22] He seems here to have copied his own earlier letter (*Le familiari*, 4.2 and Gamma) which uses the Juvenal passage as well as Cicero and Seneca. Other moral anecdotes or sayings of Socrates are added, drawn from Seneca's *Ad 'Lucillium*, Aulus Gellius, and Valerius Maximus.

It is difficult to account for Petrarch's rather conventional and not particularly enthusiastic treatment of Socrates. There are undoubtedly other references I have not cited, but those I have cited show his knowledge to have been thirdhand, deriving from Plato or Xenophon through Cicero or Seneca. But perhaps the main reason for Petrarch's

21. Ibid., 4.22; Cic. *De divin.*, 1.54.
22. *Rer. mem.*, 3.71.

lack of enthusiasm is that essentially he knows the sceptical Socrates of his Latin sources and not the religious
philosopher embedded in Plato's *Dialogues.*

With Plato himself it was quite different.[23] Petrarch
possessed the medieval Latin Plato—Calcidius's partial
translation of the *Timaeus,*[24] Henricus Aristippus's translation of the *Phaedo*, and probably the latter's *Meno.*[25] He
owned a large Greek manuscript of some of Plato's works
which he hoped to be able to read after he had learned
Greek, but this enterprise ended with the premature departure of Barlaam of Calabria. A list of its contents
reveals what he could have known had he been able to
read Greek: the *Clitophon*, the *Republic*, the *Timaeus*,
the *Critias*, the *Minos*, the *Laws*, the *Phaedrus*, *Letters*. In
addition it contained *Diffinitiones Platonis, Confabula-
tiones Platonis, Demodocus de consilio, Critias de Divitiis,*
and *Axiochus de morte.*[26] In his *De ignorantia* Petrarch
refers to this manuscript to indicate the extensiveness of
Plato's writings, disdained by his young critics as "one or
two small little books." Petrarch says with his usual
numerical looseness, "I have sixteen or more of Plato's
books at home, of which I do not know whether they have
heard the names." He also says that if they come to his
house, "these literate men will see not only several Greek
writings but also some which are translated into Latin all

23. One might say with De Nolhac (1.9) that "the need to oppose a name to
that of Aristotle, as much as the study of Cicero and St. Augustine, caused
Petrarch to grasp the importance of Plato."

24. Paris BN. lat. 6280. See De Nolhac, 2.141; Pellegrin, 98. It is no. 121 of
the 1426 inventory of the Visconti-Sforza Library.

25. See note 13.

26. De Nolhac (2.133–40, 313) discusses this manuscript and Petrarch's
efforts to learn Greek in order to read it. Pellegrin lists it (98) as no. 120 of
the 1426 inventory and as no. 463 of the 1459 inventory (310). She suggests
in n. 2 that because of similarity of contents, it may well be Paris BN grec
1807, which came from Catherine de Médicis.

of which they have never seen elsewhere."²⁷ It is question-
able whether Petrarch possessed some new Latin translations of works of Plato other than the medieval three.

Petrarch's comments on Plato in *De ignorantia* and the
Rerum memorandarum libri show great admiration. How
much did he actually know of Plato's philosophic doctrines? References to his copy of the *Phaedo* are rare.
Identifiable references usually come from Cicero's *Tusculan Disputations*.²⁸ His knowledge of metempsychosis
is not specifically related to the *Phaedo*. Comments on the
divisions of the soul are based on those attributed to Plato
by Cicero. In the *Secretum* "Augustinus" alludes to Plato's
statement of the progression of desire from sensual to
heavenly in the *Symposium* (which Petrarch could not
have read). But this alludes also to St. Augustine's discussion in the *Confessions*.²⁹ "Augustinus" also cites Plato
more directly: "For what else does the celestial doctrine
of Plato admonish except that the soul should be pushed
away from the lusts of the body, and their images eradi-
cated so that purely and rapidly it may arise toward a
deeper vision of the secrets of divinity, to which contemplation of one's own mortality is rightly attached?" This
is an authentic echo of the *Phaedo*, and "Franciscus" at
this point acknowledges that he has begun to read Plato,
but the loss of his tutor in Greek has interrupted him.³⁰ In
the *Secretum* "Augustinus" quotes the *Phaedrus*, not read
by Petrarch: the poet "beats in vain on the doors of poetry
if he is in his right mind."³¹ This is certainly a commonplace in many Latin sources.

Petrarch mentions the doctrine of ideas, which he must

27. *Prose*, 756; Nachod, 112–13.
28. *Tusc.*, 1.30; *Rer. fam.*, 3.18.5 (1.139); 4.3.6 (1.165).
29. *Prose*, 46; *Confess.*, 10.6.
30. *Prose*, 98–100.
31. Ibid., 174; *Phaedrus* 245 A.

have known from Cicero's *Tusculans* and elsewhere, in the *De vita solitaria*. But it is based on another source of medieval and early Renaissance Platonism, Macrobius's *In somnium Scipionis*.[32] Plotinus, rather than Plato, is cited, and the hierarchy of the virtues is set forth—political, purgative, purged (acquired in solitude), and the fourth and highest, "archetypal," or "exemplary." "Hence the [Platonists] hold that the three other kinds of human virtue originate as though from some eternal exemplar, just as the name itself indicates; or, as Plato would say, from the ideas of the virtues which, like the ideas of other things, he placed in the mind of God."[33] Despite his professed yearning to know Plato, Petrarch makes little use of the *Phaedo* on the questions that interested him most. He infrequently repeats even the commonplaces widely disseminated in Latin sources concerning the teachings of Plato.

Petrarch's most extensive statement about Plato runs for five pages in book 1, chapter 25, of his *Rerum memorandarum libri*, under the rubric "On Study and Learning."[34] He sketches Plato's life, drawing principally on Apuleius's *De Platone et eius dogmate*, with additions from Cicero and Macrobius. Again following Apuleius, Petrarch summarizes Plato's teachings. It turns out to be a catalogue of topics (discussed at greater length by Apuleius): matter, ideas, the world, the soul, nature, time, the wandering stars, animals, providence, fate, demons, fortune, the parts of the soul and the bodily domicile, the senses, the shape of the human body and the arrangement of its parts, the division of goods, virtues, the three kinds of minds, the three causes for seeking the good, pleasure, labor, friendship and enmity, degraded love, the three loves, the species

32. *In somn. Scip.*, 1.8; *Prose*, 340–42.
33. *Prose*, 342.
34. *Rer. mem.*, 1.25, pp. 26–31.

of human faults, the condition, customs, and death of the
sage, the commonwealth, and the republic, its customs and
best laws. In Apuleius, he says, the reader will find all
these matters treated in succinct brevity and not at all
unpleasantly.[35] It suggests the medieval taste for encyclopedic epitomes and the compilation of rhetorical *loci
communes*.

Petrarch's more pressing concern is to show Plato's
compatibility with Christianity. Unlike Aristotle, Plato
taught the creation, not the eternity, of the world (though
in this Apuleius seems to differ from Cicero). Petrarch
hoped here to cite only secular authors, but finds he
cannot and switches to St. Augustine. A question arose
that was to surface again with Ficino, Pico, and the other
Renaissance Platonists: How did Plato arrive at his antici-
pations of Christianity, and should he, rather than Christ,
be given credit for these doctrines? Petrarch cites Augustine's *De doctrina Christiana* (2.28.43) to the effect that
Plato was a contemporary of the prophet Jeremiah and
had learned of at least the pre-Christian truths of the
Hebrews on his journey to Egypt. But then he cites
Augustine's own correction of this tale in *De civitate Dei*
(8.11), where he asserts that Plato and Jeremiah were not
contemporaries and that Plato also lived before the Sep-
tuagint translation of the Old Testament had been made.
Hence these truths must have been made manifest by God
to Plato, as St. Paul argued in Romans 1:19. Thus Plato
is made the equivalent of the Renaissance Platonists'
priscus theologus, or else he discovered these truths by
colloquy with someone versed in Hebrew letters. Except
on the question of the incarnation, Petrarch advises a
reading of Augustine's *Confessions* to see the extent of
the parity between Plato and Christianity.[36] Petrarch

35. Ibid., 1.25, lines 78–94.
36. Ibid., lines 99–157.

asserts that as had been said of Carneades, for Plato there was but a single end for both philosophizing and living. This seems to have been basic to Petrarch's conception of philosophy.[37]

Petrarch perhaps most eloquently praises Plato in the *De ignorantia*. It is a rhetorical statement that does not enter into the substance of either the philosophy of Plato or of Aristotle, whom he is denouncing. Plato has been called the prince of philosophy. By whom? Cicero, Vergil, Pliny, Plotinus, Apuleius, Macrobius, Porphyry, Censorinus, Josephus, Ambrose, Augustine, Jerome, and others. Who denies this glory to him? Only Averroës. But there is also the question of weight as well as numbers. Here, too, Plato excels. "I would state without hesitation that in my opinion the difference between them is like that between two persons of whom one is praised by princes and nobles, the other by the entire mass of the common people. Plato is praised by the greater men, Aristotle by the bigger crowd; and both deserve to be praised by great men as well as by many, even by all men." Both came far in natural and human matters, but the Platonists rose higher in divine, and Plato came nearer to our goal. Hence the Greeks today call Plato divine and Aristotle "demonious."[38] Petrarch then cites the large number of books written by Plato, attested by his own Greek manuscript.

The situation with Aristotle is very different. Petrarch seems to have known both the *Nicomachean Ethics* and the *Rhetoric* fairly well, judging by the nature of his citations of them. Only one Aristotle manuscript, however, can be identified as Petrarch's own, an *Ethica* with commentaries (BN lat. 6458, with scarce annotations). This led De Nolhac to comment, "But the manuscript at least establishes, for reasons that we have said, that Petrarch

37. Ibid., lines 158–69.
38. *Prose*, 750–54; Nachod, 107–11.

studied Aristotle but little."[39] It is not certain that this is true. Petrarch at least seems to have read Aristotle and used him for a commonplace book, as he did certain Latin authors. Nor does the manuscript show the kind of overt hostility to Aristotle in the use of his sayings that other passages on him have led us to expect.

This essentially rhetorical use of Aristotle for purposes of argumentation can be seen in *Le familiari* and the *Invective contra medicum*. A key statement in the *Ethics* (1103 B 28) is that "we are inquiring not in order to know what virtue is, but in order to become good." This would seem to have found much favor with Petrarch, and he affirms it as applying to himself. Petrarch denies that Aristotle actually observes this criterion in his great polemic against Aristotle and Aristotelians, the *De ignorantia*.[40] Twice he uses Aristotle's advice that faults of one extreme must be corrected by leaning to the other, "as people do in straightening sticks that are bent" (1109 B 4-7). He does this once in admonishing the four cardinals on how to reform the contemporary Romans, and once in fictitiously admonishing Julius Caesar.[41] Aristotle, discussing deliberation as an intellectual virtue, points out that the end of the investigation is the discovery of the beginning or the first cause: "What is last in the order of analysis seems to be first in the order of becoming" (1112 B 23-24). Petrarch in a brief note to a close friend uses this statement merely to suggest that he has finally got around to writing. Just as it pleases the philosophers, he who is first in deliberating is last in performing—certainly

39. 2:152. De Nolhac discusses Petrarch's knowledge of Aristotle on 147-52. Pellegrin (115) identifies this manuscript as (293) no. 190 of the 1426 inventory and as no. 78 of the 1459 inventory (293).

40. *Prose* 744-46; Nachod, 103-04.

41. *Rer. fam.*, 11.16.35, and 23.2.42.

a loose proverbializing of an originally serious philosophical point.[42]

Petrarch suggests to a friend that the day of birth may be worse than the day of death, as the one brings sorrows and the other joys. "But lest we should depart from the opinions of the vulgar—from whom, nevertheless, if we should progress toward salvation, how far we must part—it is said that death is to be feared, and that most widely repeated saying of Aristotle is heard, 'death is the ultimate of terrible things.' " Aristotle was discussing courage (1115 A 27), and death is the greatest of the terrible things a man must face. But Petrarch adds, twisting Aristotle's meaning, "He, himself, also deliberately wished to call it, not the greatest but the last." There follows a long list of heroic ancient deaths and misfortunes to show, no doubt, how terrible is this world.[43]

Petrarch turns another citation from the *Ethics* to his advantage in the *Invective contra medicum.* His basic argument is that medicine is less honorable than poetry because it is more necessary, and thus it is comparable to agriculture. To make his point he cites Aristotle's discussion of justice, where an equality of exchange between two mutually needy persons, each of whom has something the other wishes, must take place: "For it is not two doctors that associate for exchange, but a doctor and a farmer" (1113 A 17–78). Petrarch says, "I do not wish to insult you that I place you and farmers together, Aristotle does the same. . . . I believe that on account of reverence for Aristotle you have allowed this to be suffered in silence."[44]

In our final example, Petrarch seems to have applied the

42. Ibid., 11.4.1.
43. Ibid., 3. 10. 7.
44. *Contra med.*, 3.328–35.

Nicomachean Ethics to a more comparable argument. In
Le familiari 8.3, he is discussing the relative advantages of
places to live. "The crowd thinks even philosophers and
poets are hard and stony, but in this as in so many things
they are mistaken, for they also are of flesh, they retain
humanity, they abandon pleasures. Moreover, it is a certain
measure of necessity, whether philosophic or poetic, which
it is suspected they pass by. 'Nature,' as Aristotle says, 'is
not sufficient by itself for speculation but also needs a
sound body, and food, and the other means of exist-
ense.' "[45]   So also says Aristotle in his discussion of the
greater happiness of the life of contemplation (1178 B
34-35).

⌈Petrarch cites the *Metaphysics* several times, though
entirely from book 1. Twice he interprets Aristotle as
saying that the first theologians were poets, because this
fits the notion of *theologia poetica* he is promoting in
competition with scholastic theology. In the *Invective*
the reference (to *Metaph*. 983 B 28) is vague: "Certainly
the first theologians among the pagans were poets as the
greatest of the philosophers and the authority of the
saints confirm."[46]   In the well-known letter to Gerardo
analyzing his own eclogue as a form of theology, Petrarch
first refers to the use of allegory in Scripture as poetry
and suggests that the pagan poets do the same—that is,
mean God and divine matters when they speak of gods and
heroes—"whence also we read in Aristotle that the first
poets were theologians."[47]   Aristotle, no doubt thinking
of Homer, says, "Some think that even the ancients who
lived long before the present generation, and first framed
accounts of the gods, had a similar view of nature (to

45. *Rer. fam.*, 2.159.
46. *Contra med.*, 3.448-49.
47. *Rer. fam.*, 10.4.2 (2.301).

Thales'); for they made Ocean and Tethys the parents of creation. . . ." But as E. R. Curtius pointed out, Aristotle is trying to discuss the origins of natural philosophy and not theology.[48] In the *Invective* Petrarch refers to his medical opponent's criticism that even Aristotle reprehended the poets for their arrogance which aroused the envy of the gods. This, at least, seems to be the argument he refers to. But Petrarch's answer is equally vague because, he says, he does not have the *Metaphysics* with him at Vaucluse. Petrarch does not find it agreeable to scold the poets for their liberty of speech or to excuse the envy of the gods, but he assumes his enemy does not cite this passage any more accurately than he does others.[49] Aristotle, of course, argues that the gods cannot be jealous of philosophers, as the poets suggest, since to engage in the study of metaphysics is divine and honorable because it deals with divine matters.

Whether he had his *Metaphysics* at Vaucluse when writing his *Invective* or not, Petrarch certainly knew this passage. He refers at least twice to its concluding line: "All the sciences are more necessary than this but none is better." This is a basic argument of his invective, that medicine is not of greater dignity than poetry (or philosophy) because it is more necessary, but that the reverse is true. The less the necessity the greater the nobility and dignity of an art or a science. He pursues the same argument in *Le familiari* (1.12), which according to Billanovich was apparently composed not long before the *Invective* of 1353,[50] and in which he refutes the fictitious old dialectician who argued that Petrarch's art, by which Petrarch guesses he means poetry, is the least necessary of

---

48. *European Literature*, 217-18.
49. *Contra med.*, 3.490-97.
50. *Petrarca letterato*, 1:49-50.

all. [This Petrarch gladly admits, for poetry is written for delight and beauty, not out of necessity.] His opponent's argument makes all the most sordid, necessary things the most noble. As he would have it, "Philosophy and all the other arts which in any way make life happy, civilized and beautiful, if they confer nothing to the necessities of the vulgar, they are ignoble. O new and exotic doctrine unknown also to him whose name they celebrate, Aristotle! For he said: 'Necessariores quidem omnes, dignior vero nulla.'"[51] He is equally sharp toward his medical opponent: "Impudent idiot, you always have Aristotle in your mouth. . . . He certainly did not approve of your little conclusion where he said 'All others indeed more necessary, none, indeed, more worthy! I do not indicate the place, for it is a most famous place, and to a famous Aristotelian!"[52]

Clearly, Petrarch uses Aristotle for essentially rhetorical, not philosophical, purposes. Yet he agrees with a basic philosophical attitude of Aristotle's—the superiority of the liberal arts, particularly philosophy and poetry, over the mechanical. This is specifically illustrated in the principle of the inverse ratio of necessity and nobility. Petrarch also knows and uses the *Rhetoric*, sometimes disagreeing with Aristotle's assertions. He draws on the discussions in books 2 and 3 of the emotions to which the orator appeals and of the problem of style. Petrarch particularly chides his medical foe, who professes to understand rhetoric and poetry, for his ignorance of Aristotle's *Rhetoric, Poetics*, and *De poetis*.[53] The latter two Petrarch obviously knew of but could not have seen.

Petrarch's statements against Aristotle in *De ignorantia*

51. *Rer. fam.*, 1.12.4–5.
52. *Contra med.*, 3.100–06.
53. Ibid., 2.270–81; 3.173–86.

may now be placed in better perspective. It is not so much Aristotle but the cult of Aristotle that he is attacking. All pagan philosophers are to be condemned equally for their non-Christian statements, made from ignorance. Aristotle is neither better nor worse than Plato in this respect. Petrarch revealingly says of his young friends that they "are so captivated by their love for the mere name 'Aristotle' that they call it a sacrilege to pronounce any opinion which differs from his on any matter." Petrarch's so-called "ignorance" may be due to his inadvertent differences from Aristotle, or to the problem of stating the same view with different words. "The majority of the ignorant lot cling to words . . . and believe that a matter cannot be better said and cannot be phrased otherwise: so great is the destitution of their intellect or of their speech, by which their conceptions are expressed."[54] Petrarch adds (as he did in his entry on Aristotle under "On Eloquence" in his *Rerum memorandarum libri*) that he cannot understand how Aristotle has such a bad style when Cicero had praised its sweetness. Not knowing that Cicero refers to Aristotle's dialogues, he thinks the poor quality of the translations into Latin has destroyed Aristotle's style. His contemporary Aristotelians, "whereas they can in no way be similar to Aristotle himself of whom they are always speaking, attempt to render him similar to themselves, saying that he, as a man who sought after the highest matters, was contemptuous of any eloquence, as if no splendor of speech can dwell in high matters, when on the contrary a high style is most fitting to a sublime science."[55]

The *De ignorantia* makes clear Petrarch's preference for "our Latin writers"—Cicero, Seneca, and Horace—who have "the words that sting and set afire and urge toward

54. *Prose,* 742–44; Nachod, 102.
55. *Rer. mem.,* 2.31, pp. 64–66, lines 37–43.

love of virtue and hatred of vice."[56] Despite his interest, albeit wavering, in the Greek philosophers, Petrarch fundamentally prefers the Latin tradition. He is basically concerned with rhetoric and not philosophy as we and the ancients know it.

It is impossible to review in detail the enormous influence and use in his writings of the works of the two Latins who had any claim to be called philosophers—Cicero and Seneca. In Umberto Bosco's magnificent (though still not entirely complete) index to *Le familiari*, Petrarch's citations of Cicero far exceed those of any other writer.[57] The *Tusculan Disputations* is the most cited single work of Cicero. Petrarch's interest in this work and in Seneca (and there is a marked predominance of citations from the *Epistulae ad Lucilium*) shows his concentration on consolatory Stoicism. Roman Stoicism, although differing significantly in the two versions presented by Cicero and Seneca, retains the common hortatory emphasis on the classical goal of moral autonomy. This, it seems, was central for Petrarch.

The most important idea Petrarch got from classical philosophy was the notion of pyschic and moral self-sufficiency. He could have drawn equivalent ideas from Plato's image of Socrates but did not, either through unwillingness or inability. He surely encountered the notion in the *Nicomachean Ethics*, but it was here entangled with

56. *Prose*, 744–46; Nachod, 102.
57. Citations to Cicero run to six and a half columns. The Bible and Vergil run for four and three and a third; Seneca runs for two and a third. Horace gets one and two-thirds, and Augustine one and a half. All other classical authors run for less than a column, the historians claiming a certain prominence, rightly enough, as the source for his *exempla*. Of the philosophers Plato is given two-thirds of a column and Aristotle and Socrates each one half. Cicero, Vergil, Seneca, Horace, and St. Augustine are, then, his most cited classical authors, with Cicero massively dominating. Cf. B. L. Ullman, "Petrarch's Favorite Books," *Studies*, 117–37.

the more mundane aim of securing a sufficiency of external goods to ensure the virtuous man's performance of his
moral and civic duties. Cicero's exposition of Panaetius's
views in the *De officiis* and of Posidonius's (presumably)
in the *De natura deorum* set the problem in the same
framework. Hence Petrarch's lesser use of these works.
Significantly, in *On His Own Ignorance*, he discusses the
De natura deorum, particularly Balbus's exposition of
Stoicism. But rightly unsure of how much of these views to
attribute to Cicero, Petrarch plays up the emphasis on
Providence. He fails to find in it the magnificent paean to
the rational powers of man that had once so appealed to
Lactantius and would again to Giannozzo Manetti.[58]

As Petrarch does not see this concern for moral autonomy as necessarily a pagan position opposing the Christian
doctrines of grace and justification, he comfortably engages in a series of role identifications or philosophical
experimentations. It is here that the claim that Petrarch
engages in philosophy as a poet finds its principal basis. His
doctrine of imitation—that one should penetrate to the
essence of a model and then benefit from it in a totally
original and autonomous way—is familiar. In his invectives
and his letters he sought to emulate but not ape Cicero and
thought that even in his retirement and love of solitude he
was following Cicero's example of composing his moral
treatises in his country retreats. With Seneca the role
playing becomes even more explicit, in Petrarch's conception of himself as a lay counselor and moral adviser,
particularly through his letters and in his use of the pseudo-
Senecan *De remediis fortuitarum* as a model for his own
De remediis utriusque fortunae. He explicitly played the
role of St. Augustine in the *Secretum*, but in this work it is
"Franciscus" who plays the part of St. Augustine, while

58. *Prose,* 726–40; Nachod, 79–100.

"Augustinus" is developed as a kind of Christian Seneca. Seneca is even more central to the *De vita solitaria* than the directly attributed citations indicate, as passage after passage echoes the letters and moral dialogues of the Latin sage. I have already suggested that although the evidence is not explicit, his ironic plea of ignorance in *De ignorantia* can be conceived as analogous to Socrates' profession that he was wisest of all because he knew nothing.[59]

It is particularly in connection with the *Secretum* and the *De remediis* that the question of Petrarch's concept of moral autonomy needs to be discussed. Klaus Heitmann in his study of the *De remediis* and in subsequent articles on the *Secretum* is deeply concerned with his seeming lack of discrimination between Stoicism and Aristotelianism and even sometimes Christianity, though he strongly affirms Petrarch's ultimate Christian orthodoxy.[60] So also notes Bobbio in her study of Seneca and Petrarch.[61] Yet Petrarch in his personal experience of *accidia* or despair and in his sense of its omnipresence in his contemporaries turned to the elaboration of a theology of *sola gratia*—salvation by grace alone.[62] Time and again he repudiates the classical notion, particularly as it is stated by Cicero, that man's virtuousness is in his own hands, whereas we must thank the gods, or fortune, or providence for our material well-being. Petrarch could not be more emphatic in repudiating virtue as the sole or the supreme goal in life. He does, however, see a link between the attainment of moral autonomy in this life and the desire, faith in, and hope for the grace

59. Cf. the important comments on Petrarch's role playing of the various careers he assigned himself in Thomas M. Greene, "The Flexibility of the Self," 246–49, especially 248. Greene has also written the most profound study (in my judgment) of Petrarch's theory and practice of *imitatio*, "Petrarch and the Humanist Hermeneutic."

60. See note 2.

61. Aurelia Bobbio, *Seneca e la formazione spirituale e culturale del Petrarca.*

62. *Image*, 35–41.

that can lift the Christian out of his condition of despair and grant him the necessary justification for salvation. It is the role of the writer, the poet, the philosopher, the moral counselor, the rhetor to assist the ordinary man by exposition and exhortation to detach himself from his alienating and self destructive involvement in the affairs of the world.

Reason (*Ratio*) in the *De remediis* counsels *Dolor* and *Superbia* to find their own moral center when bad or good fortune leads them to succumb emotionally with elation or fear to the uncontrollable flow of events as they impinge upon each individual. The self-integrating attitude he urges is a psychological, emotional, and moral detachment but not a withdrawal. Only the man who achieves this moral autonomy can even enter into the economy of grace and salvation.

Seneca, too, understood that the formal rigidities of Stoic doctrine were inapplicable to case after case of actual life. Like other Stoic moralists, he devised a casuistry that would alleviate the strictness of the code. In Seneca, there is a rhetorical convergence with Aristotle's more principled stress on the need for external goods. Petrarch could easily follow the example of Seneca rhetorically, as he could follow Cicero in his Academic affirmation that a rigid philosophical or moral rule was not essential.

Thus Petrarch, with all the inadequacies and defects of his knowledge of classical philosophy, managed to intuit and to adapt to the needs of his own religion and age perhaps antiquity's greatest moral insight—the ideal of self-sufficiency or *autarkeia*. In a syncretic way, Petrarch was able to unify opposing schools of philosophy, and even Sophists, rhetors and philosophers, through the writings of Cicero and Seneca. With the models of St. Augustine and St. Jerome before him, he could see how Platonism, Stoicism, and Ciceronian rhetoric could be drawn upon to serve and clarify the Christian goal of salvation. Like Augustine, he was aware of the differences between pagan and Christian doctrine and alert to the dangers of a failure to discriminate. But with his deep appreciation and understanding of this central insight drawn from classical moral philosophy, he was able to adapt, transform, and apply it to the new moral and religious situation of the later Middle Ages. Petrarch himself thus became a paradigm for posterity and thereby guided the transformation of late medieval culture into that of the Renaissance.

If Petrarch through his poetry "became a spiritual individual and recognized himself as such" (Burckhardt), he tried to persuade others to do so through his letters and treatises based on classical moral philosophy. In this way the poet became a philosopher and sought to make his own subjective insights universal. Through establishing the centrality of his own and every other man's subjectivity, he laid the basis for much of modern philosophy and spirituality—except for modern natural science, which has grown out of the great rival of Petrarch's world view, late medieval natural philosophy. The poet describing what the human condition *might be* becomes the philosopher making subjective statements concerning individuals that simultaneously acquire the nature of universals. And this is what Petrarch meant when he thought of himself as a *poeta theologicus*.

2

Petrarch and the Tradition of a Double Consciousness

Renaissance scholars have long been aware of a series of antinomies in the thought and life of Petrarch, and their efforts to interpret his works have often been attempts to resolve these antinomies. Reflecting, perhaps, the less informed and less sophisticated views of the Enlightenment and Romanticism, Petrarch was once regarded as caught between the Christianity of late medieval culture and the paganism of the classical world toward which he was clearly drawn. The previous chapter examined the attraction of classical philosophy for Petrarch; as a preliminary to a consideration of Petrarch's own late medieval and Renaissance dualities, this chapter will try to show that his ambivalences derived from those of the past and can be found in both the philosophy of Graeco-Roman paganism and the theology of St. Augustine, part of a long Western tradition of a "double consciousness."

Among the underlying causes of Petrarch's inconsistencies, more recent scholars have seen a split in allegiance between rhetoric and philosophy, between subjectivism and a desire to restore a more substantive content to thought, between Stoic and Augustinian influences, between simultaneous affirmation of salvation by free will and by grace, between medieval contemplative ideals and modern/Renaissance civic activism.[1] Attempting myself to find a resolution to some of these contradictions, I argued in *In Our Image and Likeness*[2] that Petrarch's concept of a rhetorical moral counsel, offering the aid of reason to the emotionally distressed in this life, could be reconciled with a theology of salvation by grace alone. Both were directed against the ultimate perdition that resulted from despair— Petrarch's *accidia, aegritudo, dolor*, sickness of soul.

Petrarch saw rhetoric as compatible with a fideistic theology but not with a metaphysical philosophy. Accepting Cicero's position of Academic doubt, he found rhetoric

1. Paul Kristeller has argued the importance of recognizing separate philosophical and rhetorical traditions in our considerations of Renaissance intellectual history, and he has proposed that humanism must be seen as falling primarily into the rhetorical camp. See "Humanism and Scholasticism in the Italian Renaissance," first presented as a lecture at Brown University, December 1944. Jerrold Seigel has discussed how four early humanists treated the relationship of the two disciplines in his *Rhetoric and Philosophy*. See especially his chapters on Petrarch and on Cicero (2 and 1), where he stresses the philosophical elements within the humanist tradition, a view with which Kristeller would probably not disagree. F. Edward Cranz in his "Cusanus" and his "1100 A.D." has enunciated a striking and radical thesis concerning the subjectivism of Western thinking since Anselm and Abelard, contrasting it with the late classical identification of thought and substance in the writings of St. Augustine. For Cranz, Petrarch's unconscious deviations from St. Augustine reveal how deeply his mode of thought was rooted in the new conceptions. Klaus Heitmann speculated as to why Petrarch converted the thought of St. Augustine into a heretical and Pelagian variety of Stoicism when he impersonated the saint as "Augustinus" in his *Secretum*; see "Augustins Lehre," "L'Insegnamento agostiniano," and *Fortuna und Virtus*, 56–57 and 252–59, where he discusses "Petrarcas Unterscheidung zwischen exoterischer und esoterischer Wahrheit." Heitmann's entire book is concerned with a seeming split between Stoicism and Christianity. Hans Baron has made an interesting diagnosis of Petrarch's apparent waverings between an activist, this-worldly, Roman-republican outlook and a more medieval Christian contemplative ideal with imperialist and Caesarian overtones; see his "Petrarch: His Inner Struggles." This essay will not attempt to speak directly to any of these scholars but will take as a starting point some of the considerations and questions they have raised.

2. See chapter 2, "Petrarch: Man between Despair and Grace." This argument was prompted by Heitmann and Seigel more than ten years ago.

psychologically effective but epistemologically irrelevant. Any classical or philosophical position could be validly argued for the sake of its psychological impact, but not for its truth. Hence Petrarch could borrow arguments from Stoics, Peripatetics, and Platonists with equal ease, since they could be looked upon as rhetorical *topoi* suitable to the occasion rather than eternal absolutes of rational thought. For Petrarch the Augustinian Christian, it was possible to rob the Egyptians and employ the spoil for holy ends. But his faith placed all ancient schools of philosophy, as well as medieval philosophizing, on an equal basis of unfinality. The criterion for nonscriptural and nonrevelational validity was psychological effectiveness, and the ancient Stoics, Aristotelians, and Platonists might well be superior in this regard. Contemporary Aristotelians offered no greater epistemological validity, only a rhetorically distasteful distortion of the writings of their master.

In Our Image and Likeness compared the humanist theology of faith to that of the fourteenth-century nominalist or Ockhamist school. Both the humanists and nominalists stressed the exhortation to faith and virtue as the task of the writer and thinker, philosopher and theologian. However much Petrarch, Salutati, and other humanists railed against the prattling of the dialecticians and the barbarous language of the *Brittani*, they could not conceal the fundamental similarity in the way both humanists and nominalists cast the relationship of man and God. Comparisons between the humanists and Reformation theologians also show certain structural parallels—on the one hand *sola fide* or predestination, on the other rhetoric and the exhortation of the Protestant sermon and tract to accept the Gospel or to execute the nonsaving laws of God or to trust in one's election and not despair. When this kind of sweeping comparison is brought down to cases, of course, great differences between individuals and movements appear. Nonetheless, at sufficient historical distance, this entire age can be seen to be caught up in the problem of the centrality of faith and the meaning of human thought, action, and rhetorical expression in relation to faith and salvation. Pelagians, semi-Pelagians, fideists, predestinarians, mystics, and moralists joined in a broad but intensive search for divine intimacy with a deity to whom the philosophical and rhetorical constructions of human culture no longer were thought to yield ready access.

The historical outlines of this grand spiritual search of the late medieval, Renaissance, and Reformation epochs cannot be traced here.[3] Rather, this and the subsequent chapters explore in a more restricted way Petrarch's efforts to restore the relationship of man's intellectual and artistic activities—theology, philosophy, rhetoric, and poetry— with both the spiritual reparation he saw as necessary in this life and man's needed certitude of salvation. Later chapters will set forth the thesis that Petrarch laid the basis for a new humanistic and rhetorical conception of truth, but first some of the ancient discussions of these questions will be examined both for comparison and as sources of Renaissance discussions.

In reviewing the ancients it seems best to start with Plato's confrontation of the epistemology and ethics of Protagoras with his own in the *Theaetetus*.[4] It is here we meet the "double consciousness" for the first time. In the *Theaetetus*, Plato attributes to Protagoras the famous

3. Cf. my foreword to *Pursuit of Holiness*, ix–xvii, as well as the entire volume for studies of this search.

4. Whether the ideas there presented were genuinely those of Protagoras or whether they are consonant with those presented as his by Plato in his dialogue *Protagoras*, questions on which classical scholars show extraordinary disagreement, is not of concern here. Rather, it is the position and point of view, no matter whose it is, that Plato presents as the chief competitor to his own.

saying that "man is the measure of all things," as well as the idea that man cannot find a truth beyond perception, that *sensere est intelligere*. To each man the world or any sense-object is as he perceives it; to no one is a universal truth known or knowable, if indeed it can be said to exist. Against the relativism and subjectivism of this position Socrates projected a conception of knowledge that looked toward the possession of a universal truth on which all men could, potentially at least, agree. The argument in this dialogue is complicated and perhaps incomplete, for beginning from sensation and multiple opinion, Socrates moves to the possibility of "true" or "right" opinion, which seems to be agreed-upon judgment and thus still not metaphysical, although not too different from what Protagoras thought was possible. But to right opinion Socrates adds rational definition, which, although an advance, is still not the most perfect form of knowledge, and this is as far as the argument is carried.

The problem of knowledge is discussed elsewhere by Plato, and interpreters disagree as to whether he anywhere meant to say that a man, without divine inspiration, can come closer to possession of the form or idea than an increasingly refined image of it arrived at through mathematical and dialectical reasoning. However, my main concern here is not the formal argument of the *Theaetetus*, which distinguishes two or perhaps three levels of awareness that can be entertained simultaneously, but the *Theaetetus* as setting forth the theoretical basis for the tradition of a "double consciousness."[5] Socrates offers a

5. For an attempt to examine the rather scanty influence of Protagoras on Renaissance thought, see my "Protagoras in the Renaissance." The present chapter considers some of the ways in which the hidden influence of Protagoras, along with the more overtly acknowledged influence of Socrates, reached Renaissance humanism through what I call the tradition of a double consciousness.

so-called "Apology of Protagoras" that may be taken as a fair-minded effort by Plato to state the position. In it Protagoras introduces the criterion of "goodness" as opposed to "truth." Its relevance is established by recalling Petrarch's statement that "it is better to love the good than to know the truth." The "Apology" states,

> For I declare that the truth is as I have written, and that each of us is a measure of existence and non-existence. Yet one man may be a thousand times better than another in proportion as different things are and appear to him. And I am far from saying that wisdom and the wise man have no existence; but I say that the wise man is he who makes the evils which appear and are to a man, into goods which are and appear to him. . . . Remember what has been already said,—that to the sick man his food appears to be and is bitter, and to the man in health the opposite of bitter. Now I cannot conceive that one of these men can be or ought to be made wiser than the other: nor can you assert that the sick man because he has one impression is foolish, and the healthy man because he has another is wise; but the one state requires to be changed into the other, the worse into the better. As in education, a change of state has to be effected, and the sophist accomplishes by words the change which the physician works by the aid of drugs. Not that anyone ever made another think truly, who previously thought falsely. For no one can think what is not, or think anything different from that which he feels; and this is always true. But as the inferior habit of mind has thoughts of kindred nature, so I conceive that a good mind causes men to have good thoughts; and these

which the inexperienced call true, I maintain to be only better, and not truer than others.[6]

Designedly or not, genuinely Protagorean or not, this is a statement of the assumption that has underlain the rhetorical tradition. It also comes remarkably close to the Stoic use of language to transform wrong opinion into right opinion and is compatible with Cicero's Academicism and with his moral philosophy in the *De officiis* and the *Tusculans*.[7]

Socrates also speaks on his own account in the *Theaetetus*. Twice in the ensuing elaborate and serpentine discussion, Plato has Socrates compare the orator or lawyer to the philosopher. The lawyer is concerned only with the immediate matter of winning his case regardless of right or wrong, justice or injustice, whereas the philosopher is helpless in this situation. It is when he withdraws and contemplates the general nature of justice that he is in his element: he is not at home in the city. The lawyer and orator live by the philosophy of Protagoras whether or not they are aware of it. Justice, honor, and piety, according to Protagoras's argument, "are in reality to each state such as the state thinks and makes lawful," and "the truth is that which is agreed on at the time of the agreement, and as long as the agreement lasts." So the orator or lawyer operates pragmatically within limits humanly determined or legislated, arbitrary or conventional.[8] The philosopher, then, is a man who seeks to move away from earthly things

6. *Theaetetus*, 166b–167a.

7. It is significant that Cicero actually translated Plato's *Protagoras* into Latin; the text, however, has been lost.

8. *Theaetetus*, 172a. Cranz, in "Cusanus," stresses the legislated character of truth in nominalist and Renaissance humanist thought. I believe his interpretation must be supplemented by consideration of the rhetorical and sophistic tradition in antiquity, where truth may first have been so conceived.

where all evil gathers indiscriminately and to move toward the heavenly, "to become like God, as far as this is possible."[9] Petrarch's own recognition of a bipolarity between city and literary retreat may be recalled, and his recognition that solitude is not suitable for the work of the orator and lawyer, but rather for the poet or philosopher.[10] Possibly his ambiguity about these two foci of living comes from subscribing to the two kinds of truths or consciousness that Plato was putting forth, though Petrarch never read and probably never heard of the *Theaetetus*. A little later, Plato, only partly ironically, assigns to the lawyer the capacity of arriving at "true opinion," though not knowledge, in his arguments before the law courts.

For Plato, then, there were two realms of consciousness, one inferior and one superior, one based on perception refined by measurement according to agreed-upon human judgments, the other based on an ascent toward a clearer image of the eternal forms. And the philosopher, if Socrates' position in the *Republic* is followed, must constantly seek to refine the first realm of consciousness by the principles of the second, moving it from the relative and the temporal toward the absolute and the eternal. He has a teaching and a rhetorical function (cf. *Phaedrus*) just as the orator does, but a higher, illuminated one that must lead toward the divine rather than seek the expedient within the humanly established and given of this world.[11]

It is remarkable how many ingredients of later discussions vital to the history of humanism are contained in this dialogue, and particularly how it establishes traditional lines that find renewed expression in Petrarch. At the base of Protagoras's position, according to Socrates, was the

---

9. *Theaetetus*, 176a.

10. *De vit. sol., Prose*, 362–66; Zeitlin, 154–58.

11. Cf. Plato's *Phaedrus*, 277b–279a, and his encomium of Isocrates. Also cf. *Republic*, especially books 7 and 9.

Heraclitean conception of reality as continually in flux. Thus not only are no two perceptions of the same reality identical, but the reality itself is never the same. Against this Plato projects and Aristotle creates an ontological view of reality affirming order, structure, and hierarchy. Petrarch is ambivalent about the flux of Fortune, and he uses Heraclitus in his prologues to the second books of the *De remediis* and the *De otio religioso*.[12]

Protagoras is given no concept of will by Plato, and the argument revolves around the question of knowledge. The Socratic assumption is that deep knowledge of true ends is sufficient motivation for the union of the self and the object. As I will show, this assumption is critical for the development of Augustinian epistemology. Here Protagoras substitutes the "better" perception for the truer, begging the question of whether health, political expediency, or conventional justice are in fact preferable to their opposites.

But "will" is involved in such choices whether or not it is conceptualized. Socrates offers a conflict of imitation or identification in place of a discrimination between the more and the less desirable. The wise man through his superior perceptions and conceptions will be drawn toward the divine model, the ignorant man toward the earthly model. In Greek thought, man is alternately cast in the image of the gods and the beasts. The choice rests on a particular structuring of reality and man's relationship to it, and on a kind of unuttered belief in the magic of sympathy and antipathy at work behind Plato's dialectic of the same and the other. Man's ignorance begets his dissimilitude to the divine and draws him to the lower "realm of dissimilitude." It is crucial to note that Protagoras is not a mere representative of dissimilitude but is

12. *Image*, 49.

conscientiously portrayed as having a philosophy with structure of its own, however contemptible or self-contradictory in the eyes of Socrates. It is that all men confront life and the external world as a chaos, and they do not so much discover an underlying structure (as the pre-Socratics sought) as create and impose one. Rhetorical invention is the instrument by which men transcend their isolated individual shuddering before chaos and act upon the world by collective convention, agreeing to establish the human community and give it certain standards of justice and piety, which they then enforce.

Underlying this reasoning is the idea that knowledge is an acquired art rather than an intuition of divinity. The order that men discover in the world is an order they give it through the invention and development of language. Nature is known hypothetically and empirically, as in the Sophist-influenced Hippocratic school of medicine. The same follows for the chaotically and individually perceived divine. Mankind achieves a willed social, natural, and divine order, and different communities and cultures achieve differing orders. This is in contrast to the discovery or revelation of the single, true, eternal order of Plato and Aristotle. For the Sophist, and the rhetorical tradition, civilization is this invented human order that replaces the time when men lived like beasts. Such is the basic humanist myth of civilization as found in Cicero's introduction to his *De inventione*. Protagoras's great myth of justice resting on *paideia*, as Plato narrates it for him in his dialogue by that name, should also be so interpreted.[13]

For understanding Petrarch and Renaissance humanism, the most important subsequent history of this double consciousness, these alternatively entertained versions of

13. *Protagoras*, 320b–328a, and see Guthrie, *Greek Philosophy*, 3:63–68; Jaeger, *Paideia*, 298–321.

humanitas, is Cicero's and Seneca's Stoic interpretation. Cicero ambiguously adheres to both myths—the Protagorean and the Socratic (or the Isocratean and the Platonic), which he thinks of as somehow blended and combined with Stoic thought in the contemporary Academy. In the *Tusculans*, the most frequently cited by Petrarch of all his works, Cicero's principal source seems to be Chrysippus. Though he mentions Peripatetics, Platonists, and Epicureans, his outlook is essentially Stoic and Chrysippean.[14] Cicero's discussion is of the highest significance for understanding Petrarch, for it concerns the cure of the disorders of the mind or the soul: "What diseases can be worse in the body than these two [of the soul] (as I pass over others): *aegritudo* and *cupiditas*?" These are both central problems in Petrarch's *Secretum*, and the following relates both to this work and to the *De remediis*:

How indeed can it be argued that the soul cannot cure itself when the soul has discovered the medicine even of the body and when the very constitution of the body is capable of much for bodily health, nor do all who submit to be cured grow healthy instantly but souls which wish to be cured and obey the teachings of the wise are without any doubt brought back to health? Philosophy is certainly the medicine of the soul.[15]

14. See T. W. Dougan and R. M. Henry, introduction to Cicero, *Tusc.*, 2:xxx–xlvii, for an analysis of Cicero's Greek sources and a critique of modern scholarship thereon.

15. *Tusc.*, 3.3.5–6: "quibus duobus morbis, . . . aegritudine et cupiditate. . . ." Cf. Petrarch's discussion of *rerum temporalium appetitus* in *Secr.*, book 2, *Prose*, 82–96, and of *funesta quaedam pestis animi, quam accidiam moderni, veteres egritudinem dixerunt*, ibid., 106–28. Although incorporated into a discussion of the seven deadly sins, these two drawn from Cicero occupy most of book 2.

With this conception, the philosophical schools of the
third and second centuries took over the role that Protagoras had seen as that of the Sophist. Cicero recognizes
its importance not only among the Stoics but also among
the Epicureans, the Peripatetics, and the Academics, for
he discusses and compares their cures and their ideas
about psychic disorders. Clearly, this is a different role for
philosophy than the pursuit of truth (about man, nature,
the gods). The reasoning by which this function is
accepted is crucial, and the intellectual basis for it among
the Stoics can be seen in Cicero. "There are," says Cicero,

> innate seeds of the virtues in our minds which, if
> allowed to grow, nature itself would lead us to a
> blessed life. But now at the very moment we issue
> forth into the light and are received we are continually
> involved in all kinds of depravity and in the worst
> perversity of opinions so that we seem to suck in
> error almost with the nurse's milk. When we are re-
> turned to our parents and thence turned over to
> teachers, we are so imbued with various errors that
> truth yields to vanity and nature itself to confirmed
> opinion.[16]

The function of philosophy thus becomes the correction
of the errors of opinion in accordance with the immanent
presence of truth in the mind of man, insofar as it has been
kept pure and unobscured. This variety of Stoicism certainly has Socratic roots and implies that the possession
of pure thoughts automatically brings about a condition
of pure virtue. It also can lead to that depersonalized identification of subject and the substantive world that was
the mark of late antique thought. Moreover the rival
schools had parallel ideas, the Platonists and Peripatetics

16. *Tusc.*, 3.1.2.

admitting that vices or the diseases of the soul came from the equally innate passions and could not be totally eliminated, only moderated, with the Epicureans offering contervailing pleasures to the travails of the mind. In practice the Stoics were unable to insist rigidly that all mental suffering was mere opinion, for to some degree the external condition and the suffering itself had to be accepted as real, and thus they came to a position of moderating rather than eliminating feelings and substituting good for bad opinions and emotional states. Posidonius apparently went so far as to take over the Platonic anthropology of the tripartite soul in order to make the sage's counsel truly effective.[17]

Cicero presents the Stoic theory of the cure of souls in the *Tusculans*. For the cure itself, he turns to the Peripatetics, "because Chrysippus and the Stoics when they debate concerning the perturbations of the soul are in large part concerned with distinguishing and defining these while what they say concerning what cures souls or what keeps them from becoming turbulent is very small. But the Peripatetics offer much for calming down souls passing over the thorny questions of distinctions and definitions."[18] Cicero discusses the Stoic theory of the four perturbations, which are excessive reactions to seeming external evil or good: fear, grief, lust, and excessive joy. To these correspond three constancies or good states of the soul (grief or melancholia not having any alleviating state): caution instead of fear, simple joy (*gaudium*) in place of excessive joy (*laetitia*), and most significantly will (*vol-*

17. See ibid., xliii–xlvi, for a discussion of Posidonius and Cicero's use of his ideas. Cf. Heitmann, *Fortuna und Virtus*, 97–150, for an excellent consideration of Petrarch's simultaneous Stoic and Platonic-Peripatetic views, with their classical sources.
18. *Tusc.*, 4.5.9.

untas) in place of lust (*libido*), "for nature seeks all those things which seem good and flees from the contraries."

> For this reason nature itself incites anyone who has seen an object which seems good to obtain it. When this takes place constantly and prudently, the Stoics call a seeking of this sort *boulesis* and we name it will (*voluntas*): they think this occurs only in the sage and define will as that which desires anything with reason. Moreover what is incited more violently and is adverse to reason is lust or unbridled desire and this is found in all fools.[19]

On the one hand, this theory implies that a person may arrive at either a bad or a good judgment or opinion of his experiences and that it is a duty of the philosopher to try to educate him toward the higher wisdom and the better opinion. In this sense the view and function of Protagoras has been taken over. On the other hand, the better opinion is also regarded as the true or right one. The provoking cause is accepted both as real and as something to which the person responds well or poorly. At the same time the provoking cause is also regarded as not a real evil or good but as only a seeming one.

A remedy advocated in theory is to convince the subject that the object does not exist. In practice, however, the giving of remedies amounts to toning down the real or apparent evil or goodness in the provoking cause and thus correcting an inferior opinion with a better one. As Cicero says,

> To me, indeed, one thing alone seems to contain the cause in all that reasoning which relates to the perturbations of the mind—the fact, namely, that all perturbations are in our own power; that they are taken

19. Ibid., 4.6.11–12.

up upon judgment (*iudicium*), and are voluntary. This error, then, must be removed, this opinion drawn away, so that just as things judged evil are to be made more bearable, so in good things what are considered to be great and ecstatic ought to be rendered more quiet and ordinary.[20]

The purpose seems to be to moderate, not to eliminate, and Cicero is quick to advocate the casuistic fitting of counsel to the circumstances of the person. In theory Stoic, in practice Peripatetic, in either case there seems to have been a tacit borrowing from the Sophists and the rhetors by the philosophical schools; interestingly Cicero, an orator, is doing the reverse. This is the Ciceronian effort to combine rhetoric and philosophy that Jerrold Seigel has described and discovered in Petrarch. But it should also be observed that Petrarch gets his own definition of true philosophy—that which helps men to live better lives— from Cicero's equally pragmatic conception, and that in both Cicero's and Petrarch's cases, philosophy is conceived rhetorically.[21] Of much greater significance is Cicero's (and Petrarch's) capability of entertaining one set of postulates on a theoretical level and another on the practical-remedial. Here again is a double consciousness.

Perhaps of even greater importance historically is the discussion of *voluntas*—will—which, inserted in a discussion of opinion, judgment, error, right reason, and truth, injects an entirely different psychological economy, if desire or affect in some form rather than intellection is made central to the problem of human behavior. How this could grow out of the rationalistic theories of Stoicism is a paradox

---

20. Ibid., 4.31.65.

21. If so, this reinforces the separation of humanism from natural philosophy in the Renaissance and in Petrarch, for philosophy as *magister vitae* is closely tied to rhetoric, even though originating with Socrates and Plato.

that nonetheless can be resolved. For will is basic to a conception of the ego or the self, and though the concept of will seems to grow out of the sophistic and rhetorical influence on the Hellenistic philosophical schools generally, it is in Roman Stoicism that the clearest outline of a conception of self seems to emerge.

This can be illustrated by Seneca. A short but eloquent passage in his *Epistulae ad Lucilium* runs, "I seek pleasure, for whom? For me. Therefore I am looking out for myself. I flee from sorrow, for whose benefit? For mine. Therefore I am looking after myself. If I do everything for my own benefit, I am looking after myself before all else. This quality is present in all living beings; it is not inserted but is inborn."[22] There is paradox here as well, for how can there be selfhood if the rational mind is but a part of the immanent divine reason of the cosmos? But the individual self engages in constant acts of will in striving to preserve its integrity; a pre-Christian "Pelagianism," as it were, encased in its own system of providence, *pronaos*. Double consciousness is present here: the self is most self when it tries to make its opinions and its affects its own rather than externally imposed responses to circumstances. And yet in this constructive action the self dissolves in the larger world of nature and of reason. All men, short of the sage himself, live partially in the false consciousness of the irrational affects, partially in the true consciousness of reason, trying to preserve the integrity of the self from the distractions of the external world.

Stoicism, despite the strictness of its dogmas, was itself

---

22. *Epist.*, 121.17: "Voluptatem peto, cui? Mihi. Ergo mei curam ago. Dolorem reugio, pro quo? Pro me. Ergo mei curam ago. Si omnia propter curam mei facio, ante omnia est mei cura. Haec animalibus inest cunctis nec inseritur, sed inascitur."

a syncretic school, combining Socratic elements with rhetorical assumptions of consolatory persuasion. Compromises or tolerance of opposing schools were admitted by some Stoics. Both Cicero and Seneca acknowledged that even Epicureanism possessed compatible elements, a similarity that is today far more readily recognized than in the Middle Ages or Renaissance. Posidonius combined Peripatetic and Platonic elements with original Stoic ideas, and a parallel synthesis was taking place in Cicero's Middle and New Academy, first under Carneades and then, more importantly, under Antiochus and Philo. Cicero's eclectic as well as sceptic use of philosophy in tandem with rhetoric was much influenced by his teachers—especially Posidonius and Antiochus. This tendency to regard seemingly incompatible positions as leading to a single overall view of the universe was continued in later Neoplatonism, and Plotinus accepted many aspects of Stoicism and Peripateticism.

Several aspects of Plotinus's thought are important in this regard. He had a strongly developed notion of the self and conceived of the multipotentiality of the self for living on corporeal, psychic, intellectual, and divine levels, each of which had its stage and degree of consciousness. Plotinus postulated that thought itself was *nous*, an aspect of the godhead, which the individual possessed by the arduous task of thinking on the highest level of consciousness. Divine, cosmic consciousness, just short of God's ultimate self-contained unity, was the whole of which the individual human self was a part, but without losing its selfhood except as it degenerated into the chaos of matter. Petrarch did not know Plotinus directly, but though taking some of his ideas to be Plato's, he knew something of Plotinus through Macrobius's *Commentary on the Dream of Scipio* and the *Saturnalia.* Through Cicero, Calcidius, Macrobius, and St. Augustine, Petrarch formed his idea that Plato was a philosopher closer than all the other ancients to Christian doctrine.[23]

After Cicero, Vergil, and Seneca, Petrarch was nourished primarily on the writings of St. Augustine.[24] Augustine is particularly interesting in connection with the theme of the double consciousness, for it is fundamental to the structure of Augustinian thought and is embodied in Augustine's very conception of the intertwining of the two cities of God and of man, especially during the earthly pilgrimage of the citizens of the heavenly city. Augustine has taken over the whole classical conception of the public world of law, rhetoric, the lust and struggle for power, as well as of justice and the classical moral philosophies, and identified it with the city of man in its pursuit of the many possible kinds of earthly peace. He analyzes the aspirations of the philosophers, particularly of Plato, Plotinus, and the Stoics (he knows little directly of the Peripatetics but seems to have absorbed much of their thought from Neo-platonic commentators on Aristotle). Augustine shows to what extent they anticipate Christian truth and in which respects their thought is still deeply attached to the sophis-tic-rhetorical philosophies of this world. Yet he clearly sets forth the essential ambiguity of the situation of the Christian as a *viator*. In the famous distinction between use and enjoyment expounded in the *De doctrina Christiana*[25] and elsewhere, the Christian may use the things of this world as far as necessary for the achievement of civic peace and freedom of worship but should limit enjoyment to faith and hope in the blessed life to come and the

23. It should be recalled how little Petrarch knew directly of Plato, and how he yearned so nostalgically to read his writings, though not of course learning Greek or studying very thoroughly the Latin translation of the *Phaedo* that he owned (unless, of course, he acquired it in his old age).

24. See chapter 1.

25. *De doct. Christ.*, 1.3.

charity of Christian fellowship within the church. Augustine set the problem in its broadest terms for all succeeding generations of Christians, who had to live with a double consciousness of this worldly abode, however temporary, and of the ultimate holy peace of God and bliss.[26]

Two further problems need special consideration: that of the perceptual and volitional autonomy of the individual within the providential economy of divine illumination and grace, and that of the nature of perception, thought, and will, as Augustine conceived them under the strong influence of Cicero's *Hortensius* and Plotinus's *Enneads*. Ultimately both problems merge into one.

The problems of perception, cognition, will, and faith, though discussed elsewhere, can be seen especially clearly in Augustine's early *De magistro*. Having shown that we seek to know things, not words or signs, and do this both through signs and direct observations, Augustine argues that we also believe some things that we read, for example, the Scriptures, because we have faith. But this faith ultimately rests on our capacity to consult an interior truth that exists in all men who possess minds. "Referring now," he says, "to all things which we understand, we consult, not the speaker who utters words [or the written text, of course], but the guardian truth within the mind itself, because we have perhaps been reminded by words to do so."

> Moreover, He who is consulted teaches; for He who is said to reside in the interior man is Christ, that is, the unchangeable excellence of God and His everlasting wisdom, which every rational soul does indeed consult. But there is revealed to each one as much as he can

26. Cf., e.g., *De civitate Dei*, 19.14, 17, 20, 26, 27.

apprehend through his will according as it is more or less perfect.[27]

Christ, the Logos, the divine Word, exists within the human mind itself. The capacity for thought, insofar as it is free from the distortions of a perverted will, allows one to grasp truth within one's own mind. The grace that frees the will from its corrupt attachments to lesser goods is simultaneously the divine illumination within the mind that is truth and reveals truth and grasps truth.

The identity of the subjective element of thinking with the substantial element of truth, which Cranz has stressed, could not be clearer. Nor could its Plotinian provenance be more apparent. Man learns about external things by sense perception, and this is called sensible knowledge. So also man learns from the interior light, either by reasoning or by recalling images of external things perceived; these are intelligibles. "Indeed when things are discussed which we perceive through the mind, that is, by means of intellect and reason, these are said to be things which we see immediately in that interior light of truth by virtue of which he himself who is called the interior man is illumined, and upon this depends his joy."[28] Not only in a Christian sense but in a strictly philosophical sense Augustine sees a double consciousness built around the old sense knowledge of the Sophists and the internal knowledge of ideas or intelligibles that had come down to him from Plato through the Stoics and Neoplatonists. But the internal knowledge of intelligibles seems to be identical with religious illumination, which is the reason, of course, that Augustine could make no distinction between theology and philosophy.

Augustine's eloquent description of his conversion in the

27. *De magistro*, 11.38; Leckie, 390.
28. *De magistro*, 12.40; Leckie, 391.

Confessions presents further aspects of his thought. Seated in the garden in the agony of irresolution, he suffers what seems at first a conflict of mind and body, which he comes to recognize is not a conflict of two minds but of two wills. "The mind commands the mind to will and yet though it be itself, it obeys not." This is because it does not command entirely. "It is . . . an infirmity of the mind that it does not wholly rise, sustained by truth, pressed down by custom. And so there are two wills because one of them is not entire."[29] Had there been two minds, the truth of Manichaeism would have been admitted, for the mind also represents the presence in the self of something larger originating outside it. It is the will, not the mind, that is identified with self: "I it was who willed, I who was unwilling. . . . Therefore I was at war with myself, and destroyed myself."[30] But the soul also remained one: "Thus also when eternity delights us above, and the pleasure of temporal goods holds us down below, it is the same soul which wills not that or this with an entire will, and it is therefore torn asunder with grievous perplexities, while out of truth it prefers that, but out of custom does not lay this aside."[31] "This controversy in my heart was naught but self against self."[32]

It is to this scene that Petrarch refers when describing his own supposed inner conflict in book 1 of the *Secretum*. He cites Augustine: ["At the very moment in which I was to become another man, the nearer it approached me, the greater horror did it strike into me; but it did not strike me back, nor turn me aside, but kept me in suspense."][33]

29. *Confess.*, 8.9.21; Pilkington, 122.
30. *Confess.*, 8.10.22; Pilkington, 123.
31. *Confess.*, 8.10.24; Pilkington, 124.
32. *Confess.*, 8.11.27; Pilkington, 125.
33. *Confess.*, 8.11.25 (Pilkington, 124): ". . . punctumque ipsum temporis quo aliud futurus eram, quanto propius admovebatur, tanto ampliorem incut-

Classical thought was evolving toward the position reached by St. Augustine. It was he who most clearly saw that there can be dual modes of knowledge deriving from sense perception and interior illumination, and that these modes depend for resolution and are even overshadowed by the force of will within the self. Will has become more than desire in accord with right reason, as Cicero held. For Augustine it has become the deepest and most energetic part of the self, which has grown through attachment to customary ways and even more importantly through an innate joy in and love for the truth. Thus the will can be torn in opposite directions.

Petrarch also was seeking a wholeness and integrity of the self in the *Secretum* and the *De remediis*, not only for himself but also for others. For Petrarch the transformation of the self had to come from divine mercy, by grace alone, but first there had to be a mind that knew its errors and the self-deceptions of its affective attachments to alluring but destructive ways of existence. Insight concerning the self was not enough, either for Augustine or Petrarch, but insight concerning the self was a needed preliminary to the possibility of grace. It could warn at least against the terrible dangers of despair, the *aegritudo* or grief of soul which Cicero thought could so easily be

---

iebat horrorem; sed non recutiebat retro nec avertebat, sed suspendebat." Petrarch, *Secr.*, *Prose*, 40: "'Augustinus': . . . Et tamen hec inter idem ille qui fueram mansi, donec alta tandem meditatio omnem miseriam meam ante oculos congessit. Itaque postquam plene volui, ilicet et potui, miraque et felicissima celeritate transformatus sum in alterum Augustinum, cuius historiae seriem, ni fallor, ex *Confessionibus* meis nosti." *Image*, 5–17; cf. Heitmann's articles, cited in note 1. I have argued before that Petrarch confronts will with will in the person of "Franciscus" in his dialogue, and that the Augustinian reminiscence is genuine, which might seem to undercut the argument that the "Augustinus" of the dialogue employs Stoic not Christian arguments. The dialogue indeed follows Cicero's *Tusculans* and much of Seneca, including the *De tranquillitate animae*, but their arguments are turned into Christian ones through the Augustinian context.

talked away but which Augustine and Petrarch knew from experience could not. Yet the Ciceronian reasoning served them both.[34]

Petrarch knew that the nature of experience was real and could make a difference in the psychic state of the individual. Hence the great personal authenticity of his comments on the effects of urban life and its mad drive toward accumulation, influence, and power, with the accompanying destruction of the self and its depersonalization, and the more beneficial rural or monastic environment. If he draws much of this from the pages of Seneca, it nevertheless fits the realities of his own time and is a vivid and concrete transmission and application of the classical discovery of selfhood to the modern world. There is also in his two works on literary and religious retirement, the *De vita solitaria* and the *De otio religioso*, a sense of man's double attachment to both worlds. *Otium* is conceived in the city in the midst of *negotium*. The poet in his retreat and the monk in his cell, however, have not entirely escaped corruption and the external world. The dangers remain, and Petrarch not only sides with the poet and theologian and consolatory philosopher but also sees the great importance of the orator and the lawyer who work to compose the quarrels of the town and bring decency and civilization to all mankind. Indeed, in the *De ignorantia* he abandons philosophy altogether for rhetoric and theology, as was the tendency of his age.

Hans Baron has looked for the civic moments of Petrarch's career to contrast with the solitary, medieval religious ones, but one cannot avoid concluding that for Petrarch both are parts of a whole, although in response to the still living classical and Christian double consciousness he

---

34. *Confess.*, 8.7.17; Pilkington, 120. The problem of consolation was dealt with in the *Tusculans*, where Cicero refers to his own *aegritudo* (after the death of Tullia), and how it was discussed in his *Hortensius*, the great lost work that drew Augustine to philosophy.

sometimes oscillated between them and sometimes sought to unify them. Thus, as Seigel has urged, the philosophy manifested in his meditation and in the silence of contemplation was as much soul mending as the rhetoric. Heitmann's fears for the unchristianity and heresy written into "Augustinus" by Petrarch dissolve also in this larger whole.[35]

It is not completely clear to what extent Petrarch broke away from the ancient theory of the substantiality of thought, as Cranz has argued. Petrarch admired, identified with, and attached himself to those notions of will and selfhood in Augustine that most stretched the ancient identification of world and idea and turned it toward subjective individualism which it might be claimed Augustinianism, if not Augustine, created. The crucial problem is whether Petrarch accepted the identity of illumination and grace, and therefore of intellect and will. Since he said that "it is better [or more sufficient, *satius*] to love the good than to know the truth," perhaps he did indeed break the Augustinian bond. It is difficult to imagine the great advocate of "Joy in the Truth" putting the issue exactly as Petrarch did.

But if Petrarch rejected the doctrine of the substantiality of thought in favor of subjectivity and separated rhetoric and a theology of faith from philosophy, it was in some ways a return to the more extreme ancient statements of the proponents of sophistic and rhetoric. It was a return to Gorgias, and especially to Protagoras, who asserted the primacy of goodness over truth and considered both to be subjective constructions of man. To conclude, if subjective

35. Whether Augustine himself fully transcended the "premature Pelagianism" of the Stoics or not, he certainly did not abandon the problem. His career in philosophy led him ultimately to Christianity, and he continued to urge the use of rhetorical moral injunction as a mode of religious persuasion. See *De doct. Christ.*, book 4.

self-consciousness and the controlled construction of the image of the external world we call natural science are regarded as the double ingredients of the modern consciousness, the three great rhetors who consciously transmitted the Greek and the ancient classical and Christian wisdoms to their own cultures—Cicero, Augustine, and Petrarch—have to be given much credit for their part in this historical evolution of ideas.[36]

36. As a postscript I would like to comment briefly on William J. Bouwsma's recent paper, "The Two Faces of Humanism: Stoicism and Augustinianism in Renaissance Thought," which by coincidence was apparently written at about the same time as this chapter. Although, as I have argued, both Stoicism and Augustinianism contain dual elements of tension, or dialectical interplay (as do Platonism and Peripateticism also), comprising what I have been calling a "double consciousness," Bouwsma uses these two traditions as broad labels to designate the polarities he discerns in Renaissance thought beginning precisely with Petrarch. Although his structuring of the duality is not identical with mine, it does seem to be an interesting projection forward in time of some of the same elements I have identified in the intellectual traditions preceding Petrarch (the ancient, not the medieval ones, to be sure). Bouwsma seems right in his description of the difference between his approach and mine in *Image*: "The chief difference between his treatment of the subject and my own is one of emphasis; Trinkaus seems to me primarily concerned with the humanist effort to harmonize Stoic and Augustinian impulses" (n. 1). However, the hypothesis of a tradition of a double consciousness put forth here has also tried to capture some of the ambivalence and tension and the effort to resolve it that continue on into Renaissance humanist thought. I am also quite aware that the problem of tracing and expounding ancient philosophy is extremely complex and would refer the reader to two recent and salutary surveys: the multiauthored *Cambridge History of Later Greek and Early Medieval Philosophy* and John Dillon, *The Middle Platonists, 80 B.C. to A.D. 220.*

3

Petrarch's Critique of
Self and Society

Petrarch's double consciousness of both an experienced
and a revealed truth is most acutely manifest in three
important prose works of the 1340s. In them he deals with
the question of selfhood in the context of his own age.
Casting himself in the role of moral philosopher, he draws
upon admired figures of antiquity—primarily Cicero,
Seneca, and St. Augustine, with Plato, Socrates, the Stoics,
and the Greek Sophists and the Neoplatonists standing
dimly behind his favorite Latins. Ultimately he turns to
Scripture and St. Paul. In these three works Petrarch sets
forth a view of man caught in the tension between the
eternal, divine economy of salvation regulated by the
church and a burgeoning historical world of human concerns. Two features are prominent in his approach to this
dilemma. The first is his sense of an opposition between
the religious and secular realms—life in accord with the
discovery of God and holiness versus the attainment of
worldly goals such as literary fame, wealth, romantic love,
and glory. The second feature is Petrarch's transformation
of the dilemma into his own version and would-be resolution of the double consciousness wherein the soteriologi-
cal imperatives of the higher way find their only knowable
reality and authenticity in the concreteness of individual
everyday experience.

This chapter is a revised version of my article "Petrarch's Views on the
Individual and His Society," which originally appeared in *Osiris* 11 (1954):
168–98.

Petrarch's vision of his own situation and experience, imaginatively projected in his *Secretum* (long thought to be of 1342/43, but newly dated as 1347–53), is shaped in his later writings into a basic structure of Renaissance moral and anthropological consciousness. The stance (with all its inherent ambiguities) assumed in the *Secretum* is extended from the exemplum of his own person in debate with St. Augustine (designated as "Franciscus" and "Augustinus," respectively) to the attitudes and circumstances of the urban *vulgus*, contrasted in turn with the poet's rural *otium* in the *De vita solitaria* of 1346 *seq*. It is further extended to the perils of his brother's fellow Carthusians as observed and exhorted by the now amateur theologian Petrarch in the *De otio religioso* of 1347.[1]

Datings are problematical, and none of these works was left unrevised. Although earlier manuscript versions of some of them survive, it is risky to represent them as constituting a particular phase in Petrarch's development. Much of what was clearly part of later attitudes of the fifties and sixties was written into them.[2] However, the sense of irreconcilability between the divine and the worldly modes and goals of life is very sharp in all three works. Petrarch does not think that much can be done about the morass of distracting and diverting goals, habits, and desires, yet his later works, which will be studied in the following chapters, show that he came to believe that an instrument of liberation was available. The roots of this Renaissance self-confidence were planted in these earlier writings.

Recent scholarship has emphasized the significant parallels between the rise of Renaissance humanism and

1. For full citations of these works of Petrarch, see Works Cited under "Petrarca." For established datings, see Martellotti's "Nota critica ai testi," *Prose*, 1162–63, 1166–68, 1168–69. Proposed new dates for *Secretum* in Rico, *Vida*, 9–16, "Precisazioni."

2. Cf. Bosco, *Petrarca*; Billanovich, *Petrarca letterato*.

the scholastic *via moderna* of the *nominales* of the fourteenth and fifteenth centuries.[3] Petrarch had strong views
on his contemporary seekers of truth, and the pungency of
his invective can mask shared ideas. At the same time, it
would be well to examine not only the coincidences of
humanism and nominalism but also the bases for their
persistent hostility. In the *Secretum* Franciscus exclaims,
"This prattling of the dialecticians will never come to
an end; it throws up summaries and definitions like bub-
bles and glories in matters for endless controversies, but
for the most part they know nothing of the real truth

3. Cf. Oberman, "Notes on the Theology of Nominalism," and his "Shape
of Late Medieval Thought." Oberman's recent *Werden und Wertung* seems
more concerned with stressing the independent influence of the *via moderna*
in Reformation Germany, which is fair enough. But he also reasserts the close-
ness of the *devotio moderna* to both *via moderna* and humanism contra
Post, *The Modern Devotion*. Cf. *Image*, part 1.

Parallels have also been drawn between the new modes of thinking about
the natural world that arose in the fourteenth century at Merton College, Oxford, and at Paris and the rise of Renaissance humanism, especially in Italy.
There also seems to have been an English mendicant vogue for classical studies,
possibly linked to Avignon, where Petrarch centered his life until the early
1350s. The protoscientific revolution of the fourteenth century was closely
associated both at Oxford and Paris with the nominalist school of theology,
just as Beryl Smalley's "proto-humanists" had important links with the *via
moderna*. See her *English Friars*, especially chapter 7 on Robert Holcot.

It is "premature" (to use Oberman's word—see his "Fourteenth-Century
Religious Thought: A Premature Profile") to consider the moral revolution
that Petrarch so firmly structured as part of either the broad and influential
via moderna movement or of Oberman's "Augustinrenaissance," though Paul
Kristeller has pointed to the importance of Augustine for many Renaissance
thinkers, and my own studies have reinforced that idea. See Oberman's *Werden und Wertung*, chapter 6, "Augustinrenaissance im späten Mittelalter";
P. O. Kristeller, "Augustine and the Early Renaissance"; and *Image*, part 1.
Also see Bouwsma, "The Two Faces." Renaissance humanism had many of the
characteristics of a religious movement, and if prior to sixteenth-century
Erasmianism it did not literally constitute such a movement, it manifested at
least a definite and characteristic religious emphasis in some of its leading
figures. Cf. *Image*, especially part 4, "The Christian Renaissance in Italy,"
and my "Italian Humanists and the Reformers." But note Kristeller's cautions
in "The Role of Religion in Renaissance Humanism and Platonism."

of what they are talking about." The only way to handle such vainly negligent and idly curious men is to launch some invective at them: "Why, O wretched ones, do you always labor in vain and occupy your minds on such silly subtleties? Why do you grow old among words, forgetful of things?"[4]

The occasion for the criticism is revealing. Augustinus has charged that men in general are forgetful of their mortality, preoccupied with the trivia of daily existence, oblivious of their ultimate goals. Franciscus adds that few are even aware of the hackneyed definition of man as an animal that is rational and mortal. As a tiresome subject of classroom discussion it has lost any meaning; hence his attack on the dialecticians. For this definition of man becomes the kernel of Petrarch's major assertion of the dialogue: the need for self-knowledge based on deep experience of the meaning of reason and of death. For Petrarch the relationship of words and things—the ancient issue of *verba et res*—should be one of increasingly close correspondence, and this is best attained through the arts of poetry and rhetoric. The humanist, through poetic and rhetorical insight, conceives of himself therefore as more capable of approaching the ultimate realities than the scholastic, who merely juggles verbal relationships and relies on dialectic. The humanist's conception of reason, inseparable from will, is the deep and total organization of experience. The figure of Truth, introduced at the beginning of the dialogue, stands silently by while Augustinus and Franciscus converse, but it is Augustinus's experience, which Petrarch knows through the *Confessions* and shares in this own life, that leads Franciscus to Truth. The truth he seeks is the understanding of man's potentiality both for a rational self-directed existence in this life

4. *Prose*, 52; Draper, 29–30.

and for salvation, not the natural philosopher's scientific truths concerning nature. Hence Petrarch's focus on the definition of man as a rational and mortal animal.

Petrarch's ideas can here be compared with the basic stance of the *via moderna*. Despite the fact that the position of the humanists is frequently confused with that of the so-called *via antiqua*, they and the thinkers of the *via moderna* were both deeply sceptical of metaphysical conceptions of the natural world predicated on the supernatural. Characteristic of the *via antiqua*, on the other hand—late medieval followers of such thirteenth-century paladins as Albertus Magnus (Albertists), Thomas Aquinas (Thomists), or Duns Scotus (Scotists)—was the positing of such correspondences between the structures of the divine and the natural. We should forget, however, neither the individual differences between humanists and *nominales* alike, nor that the distinction between *via moderna* and *via antiqua* tended to become blurred as individual scholastics varied in the degree of correspondence between the natural and the supernatural they were ready to concede.[5] Concerning dialectic specifically: while some later humanists claimed it as a subordinate part of rhetoric and made important contributions to its study,[6] Petrarch's hostility, in which he was followed by many other humanists, was based on his judgment that merely logical conclusions were psychologically shallow and incomplete. A deeper commitment of emotion and will that was also

---

5. See William J. Courtenay's discussion of the relationship of nominalism to earlier scholastic thought in his clarifying article, "Nominalism and Late Medieval Religion." The late Ernest A. Moody's *Studies in Medieval Philosophy, Science and Logic* is especially illuminating on the relationship of nominalist logic to medieval science and philosophy. Also see Oberman, "Fourteenth-Century Religious Thought."

6. See the contributions of Angelo Crescini, *Le origini*, and of Cesare Vasoli, *Dialettica e retorica*.

based on experience was required for a true understanding of man's nature and goals in this world and the next.[7]

Petrarch's views are set forth clearly in the first book of the *Secretum*. Through the dialogue between Augustinus and Franciscus, Petrarch presents a case history of the learning process, humanistically conceived. The lesson of the dialogue is that the eternal destiny of man's soul is also the eternal truth, so far overshadowing man's earthly concerns that it all but obliterates them. And man's true happiness and misery will follow as he either lives by this knowledge of the one true reality or is incapable of disentangling his thoughts and feelings from mundane affairs.

It is not the lesson itself, which is conventional Christian doctrine, that is significant, but what Augustinus and Franciscus are made to represent. Augustinus as the venerated and familiar church father, so well known to Petrarch through the *Confessions*, is not conceived, as is sometimes

---

7. Nominalist theology was indeed not insensitive to such spiritual concerns, and some of its adherents developed the kind of pastoral emphasis that is evident in Jean Gerson and possibly influenced Reformation theology. See Oberman, *Werden und Wertung*, chapter 3, *"Via moderna,"* and passim. Oberman stresses that Gabriel Biel, a leader of "pre-Reformation" thought, adhered both to the *via moderna* and the *devotio moderna*. Petrarch was evidently cognizant, at least in a general way, of the complex terminological arguments of the nominalists, wherein the more substantive assertions of the older schools were subjected to analyses of their meanings and, according to Petrarch, became within the culture of the schools empty formalistic repetition. See Philotheus Boehner's careful exposition and summary of Ockham's logical analysis of substantive problems in his edition of Ockham, *Tractatus de praedestinatione*. Suggestive comments on possible links between Petrarch at Avignon and northern scholastic centers are in Smalley, *English Friars*, 287-92. A clarifying discussion of *sophismata* in the circle of Richard de Bury and elsewhere is in Neal W. Gilbert, "Richard de Bury and 'Sophisms.'" Gilbert shows the linkage between "Anglican subtleties" and Ockhamist logic in the reaction to the edicts of the Paris Arts Faculty of 1339. For Petrarch's condemnation of the "sophistic" *Brittani*, see chapter 4. There does not seem to be much doubt that he had at least some notion of what was going on at Paris and Avignon.

alleged, as a coldly rational Stoic sage. Petrarch was indeed an admirer of the pagan Seneca and of the Cicero of the *Tusculans* and sees nothing wrong in using the moral admonitions of the ancient pagans. But Augustinus here is the saint who best exemplified by his own experience the difficulty of grasping the truth of Christianity in the depths of his soul and with his entire will. Franciscus just as clearly identified with the preconversion Augustine. The two figures are seen dynamically as the "before" and "after" of a single man; they are Augustine, and they are Petrarch too, as he feels he is and aspires to become; they are also potentially everyman.[8] Augustinus and Franciscus in this confrontation are respectively the man who has attained knowledge of religious truth by a long and arduous process and the man who thinks he possesses this knowledge but is still deeply involved in the concerns of the world. What emerges in Petrarch's text is the power and reality of these worldly claims, which are lesser realities than man's divine destiny, but for all that are not something one can easily turn one's back upon.

Seen in this context, Petrarch's point of view is def-

8. Augustinus is also a model for the future role Petrarch set for himself in his *Invective contra medicum* and his *De remediis* (see chaps. 4 and 5)—that of a practitioner of sacred rhetoric seeking to lift his readers to a state of spiritual autonomy susceptible of receiving grace. In this I come close to the position of Francesco Tateo, *Dialogo interiore*. But in using Franciscus as an exemplum of the spiritual condition of the *vulgus*, Petrarch necessarily builds the character out of authentic elements of his own experience. I shall therefore not follow the convention of citing "Augustinus" and "Franciscus" as the provenance of every passage quoted but will refer also, as seems appropriate, to "Petrarch" wherever either of them represents his views. Klaus Heitmann has been particularly disturbed by the seeming Stoicism of Augustinus, but I regard this as Petrarch's conviction that Senecan exhortation can well befit a Christian father's employment of pastoral rhetoric. Finally, it should be stressed that in the dramatic interplay between his two *personae* Petrarch is expressing his own conception of the double consciousness discussed in chapter 2. I cannot comment here but take notice of Rico's interesting study of the *Secretum* in *Vida*.

initely not Stoic, although he gladly uses Stoic modes of counsel. In fact the basic argument of the dialogue is stated by Augustinus in the form of a syllogism of two premises and a conclusion. But all three parts are psychological assertions, because they concern what man, under given circumstances, will do or will be able to do. Augustinus summarizes the argument thus: "Just as he who by deep meditation has discovered he is miserable will ardently wish to be so no more; and as he who has formed this wish will seek to have it realized; so he who seeks will be able to reach what he wishes."[9] Clearly Petrarch does not entirely spurn logic and formalized reasoning, as the two speakers even haggle over "premises" and "conclusions." But the meat of Franciscus's position is that men are not willingly miserable and hence cannot willingly overcome their misery; they are victims of fortune.[10]

Augustinus at this point switches the emphasis from the elimination of external miseries imposed by fortune to virtue as the true basis of happiness and vice as the obstacle to virtue. Since virtue is in man's power, "what makes me so indignant is to hear you suppose that anyone can become or can be unhappy against his will."[11] Franciscus agrees that the Stoic view, based on Cicero's *Tusculans*, is theoretically valid, but still the reality of existence intrudes, and "nothing is more distressful to bear than the inability to break the yoke of vices, although men struggle to do this through their entire life with the greatest effort."[12] For his entire life, as the spirit of Laura

9. *Prose*, 28; Draper, 8.
10. *Prose*, 32: ". . . quis tam ignarus rerum humanarum tamque ab omni mortalium commercio segregatus est qui non intelligat egestatem, dolores, ignominium, denique morbos ac mortem aliaque huius generis, que putantur esse miserrima, invitis accidere plerunque, volentibus autem nunquam?" Draper, 12.
11. *Prose*, 32; Draper, 11.
12. *Prose*, 34; Draper, 13.

can witness, he has accepted the first two steps of Augustinus's argument—meditated on death and misery and
ardently wished to overcome the latter—but in the third
step he has failed.

Augustinus then introduces the notion of a divided
self, resting on the divided will, as Petrarch encountered it
in the *Confessions*.

> There is in the souls of men a certain perverse and
> dangerous lust for deceiving themselves, which is the
> most deadly thing in life. For if you rightly fear the
> deceptions of those who live with you, because the
> authority of the deceiving ones takes away the remedy
> of caution and their pleasant voice resounds in your
> ears (neither of which is present in others), how much
> more you should fear your own frauds where love and
> influence and familiarity are so large, and everyone
> esteems himself more than he deserves, loves himself
> more than he ought, and the deceived and the deceiver
> are never separated from each other.[13]

This leads Franciscus to concede that he did, indeed, will
his own vices but has struggled—as did the young Augustine with whom he identifies—in tears and sorrow to re-
move them, but to no avail. Franciscus's self-deceptions
are seen also as a conflict of desires, passions, or wills,
chief of which is the desire for virtue, which stands in
opposition to the passions generated by the flesh. Augustinus encourages him by asserting that "the desire for
virtue is itself a large part of virtue."[14]

Perhaps this statement should be compared to the
famous formula of the nominalists: God will not withhold
his grace from those who "do their very best" (*facere*

13. *Prose*, 36; Draper, 15–16.
14. *Prose*, 44; Draper, 24.

quod in se est).[15] *Desiderium virtutis, pars est magna virtutis* could well have the same connotation. But Petrarch has not talked of grace. Here he presents the *desiderium virtutis* as something that must have great power and depth within the soul so as to drive out all other desires. Augustinus says that he is trying to teach Franciscus to hope and fear, a repeated and key pair of emotions in Petrarch, one of them a theological virtue. They are also one of the two Stoic pairs of affects: joy and sorrow, hope and fear. The hope here is that the desire for virtue will be powerful enough to attain its goal; the fear is that it will not; beyond these lies salvation or perdition. There is an obvious conflation of Stoic doctrine and Christian Augustinianism in this, and it will lead to Augustinus's *hope* that Franciscus can overcome the conflict of desires. Franciscus's *fear* and ultimate declaration that it cannot follows. Augustinus presents the alternatives: "Unless these passions have ceased, that desire will not be full and free; for it is necessary that as much as the soul is lifted toward heaven by its own nobility, so much is it weighed down by the mass of the body and earthly attractions; thus while you both desire to ascend and to remain below, you will fulfill neither, drawn in opposite directions."[16]

The problem is how to resolve this double consciousness and affective ambivalence. Augustinus offers a remedy—continual meditation on death and the perpetual recollection of man's mortality. It is at this point that the scholastic definition of man as a rational and mortal animal is brought forth, together with the denunciation of dialectic.[17] The recommended meditation is to be frequent and

15. Cf. Oberman, *Harvest*, 129–45.
16. *Prose*, 46; Draper, 25.
17. *Prose*, 48–58; Draper, 27–35. Cf. *Image* 11–14. See p. 55.

graphic so that the details build into an overwhelming image of reality that impresses itself deeply on man's consciousness. Petrarch's use of rhetoric and poetic imagery as a means to this end should be noted.

> We must picture to ourselves the effect of death on each several part of our bodily frame, the cold extremities, the breast in the sweat of fever, the side throbbing with pain, the vital spirits running slower and slower as death draws near, the eyes sunken and weeping, every look filled with tears, the forehead pale and drawn, the cheeks hanging and hollow, the teeth staring and discolored, the nostrils shrunk and sharpened, the lips foaming, the tongue foul and motionless, the palate parched and dry, the languid head and panting breast, the hoarse murmur and sorrowful sigh, the evil smell of the whole body, the horror of seeing the face utterly unlike itself—all these things will come to mind and, so to speak, be ready to one's hand, if one recalls what one has seen in any close observation of some deathbed where it has fallen to our lot to attend. For things seen cling closer to our memory than things heard.

To make death thinkable, Augustinus, before this passage, had demanded thoughts that would sink down deep into the heart (as contrasted with the superficiality of dialectic). He adds at the end, "This, therefore, is what I called 'to descend sufficiently deeply'—not as when perchance you mention 'death' by force of habit, or you repeat, 'nothing more certain than death, more uncertain than the hour,' and other sayings of this sort in daily usage. For they fly right past; they don't sink in."[18]

18. *Prose*, 54–56, at end: "Hoc est igitur quod 'satis alte descendere' dicebam, non dum forte consuetudinis causa mortem nominatis, dum 'nil morte certius, nil hora mortis incertius' ceteraque huius generis usu quotidiani sermonis iteratis. Pretervolant enim illa, non insident." Draper, 32–33.

Augustinus continues with another graphic passage to illustrate an effective meditation on the terrors of Hell. "Here is a test which will never play you false: every time you meditate on death without the least sign of movement, know that you have meditated in vain, as about any ordinary topic. But if in the act of meditation you find yourself suddenly grow stiff; if you tremble, turn pale, and feel as if you have already endured its pain, . . . then you may be assured that you have not meditated in vain." It is thus that man should learn that he is truly mortal (and thus confirm a part of the discussed definition of man).[19] Reason, the other characteristic of man's nature, is similarly put to the test:

> If you see a man so powerful (*pollens*) in reason that he organizes his life according to her, that he subjects his desires solely to her, that he controls the movements of his soul by her restraint, that he understands that through her alone he is distinguished from the fierceness of the brutes, and that he understands that only according to reason does he merit this name of man, . . . then, at length, he may be said to have a true and fruitful idea of that definition of man.[20]

The negative of this existential definition of the self is set forth as well. Franciscus claims that he engages in full and daily meditation on death, which he regards as probably imminent, but wonders what yet holds him back from that *integer animus* he hopes to attain.[21] Augustinus

19. *Prose*, 56–58; Draper, 34–35. Petrarch offers in this dialogue not only an alternative to dialectical wordiness concerning sin and salvation but a literary inducement to contrition in place of the priestly discipline in the sacraments of penance and extreme unction. For a penetrating study of late medieval ecclesiastical conceptions of how to administer penance, see Thomas N. Tentler, *Sin and Confession*.

20. *Prose*, 52–54; Draper, 31.

21. *Prose*, 46; Draper 25–26.

offers encouragement that anyone who so contemplates death should never "be doomed to death eternal" but concedes that something must still be wanting.[22] He makes an observation that can be recognized as Petrarch's amalgam of his reading of Augustine and the Latin Stoics.[23] Here is Petrarch's truth held in double consciousness:

> Thus in fact innumerable shapes and images of visible things, which entered by the bodily senses, after they have entered one by one, are pressed together into a mass and condensed in the penetralia of the soul; the latter, neither born for this nor capable of so many deformed things is weighted down and confused. Hence this epidemic of phantasms, dispersing and shattering your thoughts with an array of deadly concerns blocks the road to the clarifying meditations by which the soul ascends to the one, only and supreme light.[24]

22. *Prose*, 62; Draper, 41.

23. Petrarch is aware of how much his ideas seem to derive from Augustine's adaptation of pagan philosophy. Referring to his *De vera religione*, Augustinus explains, "And yet in this book, though it might be more becoming to a teacher of catholic truth for the words to sound otherwise, you will find for the most part there is philosophic doctrine, especially Platonic and Socratic," and he claims to have been inspired by Cicero's famous statement in the *Tusculans*, "They can see nothing with the soul and refer everything to the eyes; yet it becomes a man of great intellect to recall his mind from the senses and to guide his thoughts away from established custom." *Prose*, 66; Draper, 44; *Tusc.*, 1.16.37–38.

24. *Prose*, 64–66: "Conglobantur siquidem species innumere et imagines rerum visibilium, que corporeis introgresse sensibus, postquam singulariter admisse sunt, catervatim in anime penetralibus densantur." Draper, 43. The passage echoes Augustine, *Confess.*, 10.8, but Augustine's intent was very different from Petrarch's, for he wished to show the wonders of the inner world of memory. Petrarch was very familiar with the passage, as his famous quotation from it, supposedly on top of Mt. Ventoux, shows; see *Rer. fam.*, 4.1.

Franciscus's inability to attain happiness is now conceded to be a consequence of this general human condition, and Petrarch closes the first dialogue of the *Secretum* with a description of Franciscus's state of mind: "And there comes to pass that inward discord of which we have said so much, and that worrying torment of a mind angry with itself; when it loathes its own defilements, yet cleanses them not away; sees the crooked paths, yet does not forsake them; dreads the impending danger, yet stirs not a step to avoid it."[25]

After reviewing the seven deadly sins and Petrarch's culpability, the second and third dialogues take up more specific aspects of Fransciscus's state of soul.[26] One of these is the disease or sin of *acedia*. Originally *acedia* was the monk's inability to make spiritual progress, but Petrarch has in mind the disorders of the layman. He identifies *acedia* as Cicero's *aegritudo* in the *Tusculans*. For Petrarch it is the inability to break free from a depression that seems to cherish and cling to its own suffering. Later in his *De remediis* it became generalized *dolor*—the exaggerated affective reaction to misfortune.[27] He describes it thus:

> In such times I take no pleasure in the light of day, I see nothing, I am as one plunged in the darkness of Hell itself, and seem to endure death in its most cruel form. But what one may call the climax of the misery

25. *Prose*, 68; Draper, 46.

26. Petrarch's imitation of the confessional is totally self-conscious. The seven deadly sins of his list are: pride (considered a major fault), envy (not very serious), avarice (from which he suffers), ambition (admitted but resisted), gluttony (innocent of this), anger (is under control), and lust (a serious problem, but discussion is postponed to book 3). *Prose*, 68–104; Draper, 47–84.

27. On *acedia* cf. Siegfried Wenzel, *The Sin of Sloth*, and Susan Snyder, "The Left Hand of God." Also Heitmann, *Fortuna und Virtus*, 202–04, passim.

is, that I so feed upon my tears and sufferings with a
morbid attraction that I can only be rescued from it by
main force and in spite of myself.[28]

Petrarch attributes this malady to Franciscus's discom-
fiture at his dependence on external vicissitudes, on
"fortune." He shows clearly his awareness of a connection
between inner psychic disorder and the relation of an individual to society. He has Augustinus accuse Franciscus of
being annoyed with fortune, of disappointment over his
failure to realize all his ambitions in competition with
other men, of a desire for an impossible stability and
security. The connection he sees is not the external, adven-
titious one that he deduced. Instead, the impact of external frustrations on his feelings is presented in a very vivid
and concrete description:

> Every time that fortune pushes me back one step, I
> stand firm and courageous, recalling to myself that
> often before I have been struck in the same way and
> yet have come off conqueror; if, after that, she deals
> me a sterner blow, I begin to stagger somewhat: if
> then she returns to the charge a third and fourth time,
> driven by force, I retreat, not hurriedly, but step by
> step, to the citadel of reason. If fortune still lays
> siege to me there with all her troops, and if, to reduce
> me to surrender, she piles up the sorrows of our human
> lot, the remembrance of my old miseries and the dread
> of evils yet to come, then at last, hemmed in on all
> sides, seized with terror at these heaped-up calamities,
> I bemoan my wretched fate, and feel rising in my very
> soul this bitter disdain of life . . . In my case there is
> no wound old enough for it to have been effaced and
> forgotten; my sufferings are all quite fresh, and if

28. *Prose*, 106; Draper, 84–85.

anything by chance were made better through time, fortune has so soon redoubled her strokes that the wound has never been perfectly healed over. I cannot moreover rid myself of that hate and disdain of our life which I spoke of. Oppressed with that I cannot but be grieved and sorrowful exceedingly.[29]

If "fortune" is looked on as the fate accorded the individual in an increasingly competitive and unstable economic and social situation, Petrarch's diagnosis of his ills and his assignment of their origin to fortune takes on concrete meaning. The fact is, he says, that his life is not his own; he does not have the autonomy and control over his own existence, the independence that competitive social relations cause him to want. However, Augustinus offers several remedies for Franciscus's melancholic reaction to fortune. First, Franciscus should not make an exception of himself; if other people have these problems, why should he make such a fuss about the inevitable.[30] But mention of the troubles of others only provokes Franciscus to further complaints about the difficulties of city life—a favorite subject of Petrarch. Finally, Augustinus turns to another familiar plea: "If, however, the tumult of your mind within should once learn to calm itself down, believe me this din and bustle around you, though it will strike upon your senses, will not touch your soul."[31]

29. *Prose*, 106–08; Draper, 85–87.
30. *Prose*, 116; Draper, 94.
31. *Prose*, 120; Draper, 98. This statement, upon which I have commented in the text, also needs to be brought into relationship with the earlier tradition of a double consciousness set forth in chapter 2. Whereas the earlier and ancient views saw the inner calm Petrarch seeks as deriving from the mind's conjunction with external beings, Petrarch, as Cranz suggests in "Cusanus," now makes the more fundamentally modern distinction between a self-controlled and inner consciousness and one that is too emotionally labile and dependent on sensuous experience of the external world. The categories are old, but the structure of relationship of self, society, and divinity is new.

Basically, Augustinus's admonition amounts to an acceptance of the state of the world and society as inescapable and to an insulation of the individual's real life goals from his external behavior. Then if he is still miserable, he has nothing to blame but his sins. Suffering and frustration are not to be regarded as the ordinary conditions of men under specific social circumstances; they are internal moral and psychological conditions for which the individual himself is responsible. Petrarch would have liked to believe this. But the urban world offered joys as well as frustrations, and its effects could be controlled by departure or inner calm. Augustinus urges him to think of his good fortune:

> Assuredly, if you look carefully at the lives of others as well as your own, and reflect that there is hardly a man without many causes of grief in his life, and if you except that one just and salutary ground, the recollection of your own sins—always supposing it is not suffered to drive you to despair—then you will come to acknowledge that Heaven has assigned to you many gifts that are for you a ground of consolation and joy, side by side with that multitude of things of which you murmur and complain.
> As for your complaint that you have not had any life of your own and the vexation you feel in the tumultuous life of cities, you will find no small consolation in reflecting that the same complaint has been made by men greater than yourself, and that if you have of your own free will fallen into this labyrinth, so you can of your own free will make your escape. If not, yet in time your ears will grow so used to the noise of the crowd that it will seem to you pleasant as the murmur of a falling stream. Or, as I have already hinted, you will find the same result easily if you

will but calm down the tumult of your imagination, for a soul serene and tranquil in itself fears not the coming of any shadow from without and is deaf to all the thunder of the world.[32]

Petrarch was inclined to accept the idea behind this advice, and he did not lightly reject it. However, he was not as confident as Augustinus that the individual could escape the tumult and troubles of society by closing his mind to them.

In the third dialogue, when told that he is really bound to his misery by "fetters of gold," Franciscus asks, "Do you mean to tell me my soul is still bound by two chains of which I am unconscious?"[33] The first chain was his "love" of Laura. This is analyzed with great skill and real humility, presenting Franciscus as refusing at first to see anything but the noblest emotions in his love but finally admitting that it was a focus and a stimulus of his worldly ambitions. The name Laura led him to the anachronistic pursuit of the laurel with which he was once crowned. In the end Augustinus leaves his exalted detachment and gives Petrarch sound advice on how to forget her. Unconsciously Petrarch lets his real worry, that he has been a fool and appears foolish, show through. So forgetting his austerity, Augustinus tells him, "if I see at all truly, a man should guard his reputation, if only that his friends may be spared the shameful necessity of telling lies. All the world owes this to itself, but especially such a man as yourself, who has so great a public to justify, and one which is always

---

32. *Prose*, 126; Draper, 103–04. It must also be recognized that this passage has a close relationship to Petrarch's later position in the *De remediis* and the *Contra medicum* where he endorses the curative power of rhetoric, a view for which Augustinus is here the spokesman. Cf. Heitmann, 223–41.

33. *Prose*, 130; Draper, 108–09.

talking about you."[34] This concern for his public leads
Petrarch to the other chain that binds him, "glory," and
he promptly has the saint say, in some contradiction to
the advice just given, "Now I submit to you that reputation is nothing but talk about someone passing from
mouth to mouth of many people. . . . It is but a breath, a
changing wind; and what will disgust you more, it is the
breath of a crowd."[35]

In Petrarch's eyes the most serious aspect of the charge
that he is pursuing worldly fame lies in the danger that
his concern for what others think will distract him from
genuine self-realization: "You write books on others, but
yourself you quite forget."[36] Augustinus has much more
to say as to the temporary and fragile character of fame.
However, on this score Petrarch remains unshaken: "My
principle is that, concerning the glory which we may hope
for here below, it is right for us to seek while we are here
below. One may expect to enjoy that other more radiant
glory in heaven, when we shall have arrived there, and
when one will have no more care or wish for the glory of
the earth."[37] His wish is, if possible, to make the best of
both worlds. Indeed, Petrarch can find no other way
of solving this problem except by such a double standard.
Augustinus's warnings that earthly success may jeopar-
dize the heavenly finally becomes very feeble: "I will
never advise you to live without ambition; but I should
always urge you to put virtue before glory."[38] But Petrarch refuses to choose. "I will attend to myself as much
as I can and gather up the scattered fragments of my

34. *Prose*, 182–84; Draper, 160.
35. *Prose*, 190; Draper, 167.
36. *Prose*, 192; Draper, 170.
37. *Prose*, 198; Draper, 176.
38. *Prose*, 204; Draper, 182.

soul. . . . But even as we speak a crowd of important affairs, admittedly mortal, awaits my attention."[39] And so Petrarch leaves the conflict between the pressures of society for worldly success and his need for spiritual development unresolved.⌐

Psychological withdrawal could not overcome Petrarch's feelings of estrangement between his true self and the pressures of society. And even though he resigned himself to his malady and the divided existence and consciousness that correspond to it in this debate, the problem continued to be a pressing one for him, although he treated it more perceptively in other, possibly later, writings.

Shortly before or a few years after he had embarked on the *Secretum* and its revisions, he began composing his *Life of Solitude* (1346–1366). The offer of the position of apostolic secretary, which he refused, prompted him to write this defense of a withdrawal from conventional social responsibility. In this treatise his thought comes to be even more decisively individualistic, and the moral problems are more explicitly and objectively dealt with. Much of the work is concerned with the problems of his own profession as a humanist. In the *Secretum*, Petrarch had graphically described his aversion to city life, with its

. . . streets full of disease and infection, dirty pigs and snarling dogs, the noise of cartwheels grinding against the walls, four-horse chariots come dashing down at every cross road, the motley crew of people, swarms of vile beggars side by side with the flaunting luxury of the wealthy, the one crushed down in sordid misery, the other debauched with pleasure and riot; and then the medley of characters—such diverse roles in life—

39. *Prose*, 214; Draper, 191.

the endless clamor of their confused voices, as the passersby jostle one another in the streets.[40]

In the *De vita solitaria* he restates the ancient literary theme of the contrast between the moral degradation and misery of the businessmen and the idyllic rural life. He offers as well a picture of the problems confronting the intellectual, the artist, the man of letters, the clergyman, or any man with a serious profession.

Petrarch was keenly aware of his own plight as a writer and thinker. He believed that many forms of corruption develop when the intellectual professes independence but has to serve others' interests in order to live. For him the chief source of corruption was the conversion of human knowledge and culture into mere things that could be bought and sold as commodities for material gain. And since culture could not be detached from the men who possessed it, they too became commodities. They were selling the highest and most valuable portions of their personalities and activities.[41] Petrarch sees that the commercialization of culture has even become open and accepted.

> To these men (who are a great crowd in these days) letters are not the light of the mind and the delight of life but instruments for acquiring riches. Children are sent by their parents to study literature not as to an academy but as to a market-place, at great expense to the family but with the hope of much greater financial return, so that it need be no occasion for surprise if they make a venal and an avaricious use of an education which they have pursued for purposes of sale and on which they have based the sinful expectation of a usury not of a hundred percent but of a thousand.[42]

40. *Prose*, 120; Draper, 97.
41. *Prose*, 292; Zeitlin, 30.
42. *Prose*, 330: ". . . litere non animi lux atque oblectatio vite sunt, sed instrumenta divitiarum. . . . pueri a parentibus non quasi ad liberale gymnasium, sed velut ad servile mercimonium destinantur. . . ." Zeitlin, 132.

The most debilitating aspect of this culture market, however, was the effect of the sale of talent on the seller himself.

> They can claim nothing as their own. Their house, their sleep, their food, is not their own, and, what is even more serious, their mind is not their own. They do not weep and laugh at the promptings of their own nature but discard their own emotions to put on those of another. . . . To express my opinion of these men in a few words, I call them the most profoundly unhappy of all unhappy men in the world, because they are not even permitted to enjoy the brief reward of their evil practices. They have lived at the behest of another but are doomed to die at their own peril; they have toiled for the benefit of others but have incurred the sin for themselves.[43]

Some men argued that while selling their ability to speak and write they taught high moral and social purposes, and in any case, it was immoral to withdraw from social usefulness. Petrarch is quick to deny this and calls attention to the bad effect on the preacher or orator of confusing words with morality. As he had attacked the emptiness of dialectic in the *Secretum*, so in this work he even more drastically criticizes the preacher or orator who shines in his eloquence but fails in his own morals and is ineffectual in the moral and religious edification of others.

> . . . The physician is not necessarily in good health when he helps the patient with his advice; in fact he often dies of the very ailment which he has cured in others. I do not disdain the careful choice and artful

---

43. *Prose*, 318-20: "Omnia illis aliena sunt: alienum limen, alienum tectum, alienus somnus, alienus cibus, et, quod est maxima, aliena mens, aliena frons: non suo iudicio flent et rident, sed abiectis propriis alienos induunt affectus; denique alienum tractant, alienum cogitant, alieno vivunt." Zeitlin, 122-23.

composition of words continued for the salvation of
men, and I honor the useful work regardless of the
character of the workman, but this is a school of life
and not of rhetoric, and our thoughts are now fixed
not on the vain-glory of eloquence but on the secure
repose of the soul.[44]

Petrarch is equally doubtful about how much rhetoric can
do for others.[45]

Petrarch outlines the ideal life that would replace the
moral degradation of the man, particularly the professional
intellectual, who by involving himself in employment and
social activity has sold his creative self to another. Regula-
tion of one's own activities, freedom from involvement in
the whims of others, detachment from society and humanity to the degree that the individual wishes—these conditions of personal freedom seem the most desirable to
Petrarch. A contemplative intellect can best be nourished
in solitude: "We should run away from the plagues which
we are unable to drive off. And for this purpose I know
only of the haven and refuge of the solitary life."[46]

But Petrarch presents his negativism and lack of social
responsibility too strongly; he clearly has concern for his
fellowman. The Christian ethic was to love one's neighbor,
and the church emphasized charity as the road to salvation. Philosophy claimed that man is by nature social.
Considering this, could a life of isolation and solitude or
moral withdrawal be justified ethically or religiously?[47]
Feeling, however, that he can do nothing for others,

44. *Prose*, 322–24; Zeitlin, 126.
45. *Prose*, 328; Zeitlin, 129.
46. *Prose*, 404; Zeitlin, 149–50.
47. *Prose*, 322: "Quid enim, quid aut homine dignius aut similius Deo est,
quam servare et adiuvare quam plurimos? Quod qui potest et non facit, pre-
clarum mihi quidem humanitatis officium abiecisse, et ob rem hominis no-
men ac naturam amisisse videbitur."

Petrarch can give an ethical and religious justification for social withdrawal. From this viewpoint it would even seem that morality and religion may be possible only on an individualistic basis. Charity and the ethic of neighbor-love become remote, perhaps an illusion.

> I would admit . . . that whoever is in a place of safety sins against the law of nature if he does not offer what aid he can to the struggling. But for me, who have hitherto been struggling as in a great shipwreck, it is enough to pray for the aid of Him who is alone able to provide aid in our need. . . . I could wish to have everybody, or at least as many as possible gain salvation with me. But in the end what do you expect me to say? It is enough for me, yea a great cause for happiness, if I do not perish myself. But for those who profess themselves guardians of the helpless sheep, alas, how much I fear that they are wolves eager to rend them alive.[48]

This is personal religion with a vengeance. In place of the calloused self-seeking single-mindedness of the man of the world which he condemns, Petrarch substitutes a religious egoism. Despite his protestations of hope that others may be saved, it is clear that he is not greatly concerned with any general salvation, but with his own spiritual fate. In actual life, as he viewed it, the possibility of significant self-development through love of neighbor and love of God, such as St. Bernard and other medieval moralists had outlined, hardly existed. If one cannot in fact serve one's fellows for love, not profit, the golden rule becomes a hollow profession. Petrarch will not pretend to be un-

---

48. *Prose*, 328: "Cuperem magna, sed modicis contentabor: vellem cum omnibus salvus esse, si minus cum multis; ultimo quid expectas ut dicam: michi si non pereo satis est, multum est, abunde, feliciter?" Zeitlin, 130.

selfish. Moreover, he even gives up the hope that by serving others he may advance his private welfare. The ethical term is thus dropped out of the Christian's relationship with his fellows. Now only the relation between man and God is important.

> For from great love and unremitting faithful service there grows up an intimacy between God and man such as is not known between man and man. Therefore, just as it is my faith that the restless men who are always entangled in worldly troubles and completely immersed in earthly affairs are already having a foretaste of their activities in the life immortal and of the labors of Hell, so I believe it to be equally true that the solitary souls who are the friends of God and habituated to pious moods begin in this life to feel the delights of the life eternal. Nor should I say that it was beyond belief that any one of their number, to whom there clings no trace of the dust of this world, should be raised up with the assistance of that divine mercy to such a height that, though still confined to earth, he may hear the chorus of angels singing harmoniously in Heaven and behold in an ecstasy of mind what he is unable to express when he comes back to himself. But what can I know or say about all these things, unhappy sinner that I am, dragging about with me the ball and chain of my iniquities?[49]

He identifies neither with the harassed and wicked man of the world nor with the saintly recluse. For himself and

---

49. *Prose*, 352–54; Zeitlin, 148–49. Although he disclaims it for himself, Petrarch clearly accepts the authenticity of the mystical experience, perhaps even of the contemporary "Friends of God" (*solitariis Dei amicis*), any one of whose number *videat in excessu mentis quod ad se rediens non possit exprimere*. Similarly those totally involved in earthly affairs, he believes, *inferni laboris habere primitias*.

others like him he sees a middle course of piety and a quiet life as the real solution to the dilemma of being unable to live according to either path. If he listened to the heart rather than the tongue of the promiscuous preacher, he would hear "his naked conscience honestly confessing that happiness consisted not in sounding words, but quiet deeds, and in the inward possession of truth rather than in the applause of strangers or in fragile reputation."[50] In this sentiment, which is consistent with his concern for meditative truth and professional integrity, Petrarch leads the way for other religiously oriented Italian and northern·humanists and reformers. That such an attitude lay at the heart of his thinking about self and society is indicated by the fact that he does not have literal solitude in mind as an alternative to a corrupting social life. Solitude was a means through which the values he sought might be cultivated, but certainly not the only means.[51] Moreover, in the *Secretum*, Petrarch noted in his own case the failure of solitude as a way of avoiding excessive ambition.[52]

Petrarch therefore sought another alternative to the practice of a profession for its material rewards. His solution was to combine an active secular life with fidelity to oneself. This is expressed in one of the earliest expositions of what is known today as lay piety. Petrarch suggests finding a way of life that fits one's character as a means to piety. In the proper choice of a career he hopes to achieve integrity and self-direction.[53] It is the alien character of his work that prevents the individual from developing the potentialities of his nature. Pessimists suggest that these

50. *Prose*, 326; Zeitlin, 128.
51. *Prose*, 554–56: ". . . volo solitudinem non solam, otium non iners nec inutile, sed quod e solitudine prosit multis." Zeitlin, 290.
52. *Prose*, 96; Draper, 74.
53. *Prose*, 332: ". . . ab ineunte etate circa unum aliquod vite genus apprehendum quisque nostrum accuratissime cogitaret." Zeitlin, 133.

potentialities can be not only suppressed but destroyed. But Petrarch holds out hope for a remedy.

> In every well-ordered plan for reforming one's life . . . we are to follow not the road which looks most attractive but the one which is best suited to our needs. In this connection I require that a man shall be particularly honest and exacting in passing judgment on himself and not prone to be led astray by the elusive temptations of eye and ear.[54]

He has little confidence in the individual's powers to discern the right road, and many who have found it have done so only because of divine aid.

> If a man has been illumined by the celestial light at his very entrance into life, when, as I have already said, not a spark of judgment is active, and has been able to find a safe road or one whose dangers are slight and easily avoided, he has reason for everlasting gratitude to God. For one whose fortune has been less auspicious greater trouble is in store.[55]

Petrarch's doctrine of "vocation" suggests a comparison with Luther's. The latter's position was that a man could serve God in any calling, not only in the specifically religious vocations of the regular clergy. Petrarch differs by thinking that the calling must be the right one for the individual, corresponding to his nature and disposition. There is more life and tension in his view, because he recognized that often one is not so much "called" as thrust into a kind of work by "nature or accident or some mistake." One might be said to serve one's salvation, and

54. *Prose*, 334; Zeitlin, 134. See chaps. 4 and 5 for his efforts to develop a fitting remedy.
55. *Prose*, 332; Zeitlin, 133.

hence God, where the potentialities of one's earthly nature were fulfilled. Like Luther, however, Petrarch regards it as primarily in the hands of God whether one is rightly called or not. He is aware that one may not be,[56] and unwilling to trust divine providence completely, he develops his ideal in terms of a human and moral independence that must be superior to the accidents of circumstance and the compulsions of social necessity. He does not wish to stand in judgment over the consciences of others. The individual must, however, seek piety in his vocation, whether rightly and freely chosen or not: "All who have determined to lead their life, in whatever calling, out of reach of ill report, must at least keep free from indecency and sordidness which are generally found in low conditions. To avoid indecency is a duty, to have high aspirations is virtue, to attain it is felicity."[57]

It is difficult to see how Petrarch expects very many men to achieve the highest stage of identity between their way of life and their desires or character. Indeed, he feels that city life as such produces an aimlessness and inconstancy that makes all men caught within it miserable. He wavers in his views from the position that men can, if they will, find their true purpose and achieve some degree of moral autonomy to the position that the vast majority can have it neither in their power nor in their will to choose a desirable way of life: "They do not know what to do, and

56. For a comparison of the Renaissance concept of *ingenium* and the Reformation doctrine of *vocatio*, see Richard Douglas, "Talent and Vocation."

57. *Prose*, 340: ". . . ad fatendum multi, ad credendum nemo cogitur. Nulla maior quam iudicii libertas, hanc itaque michi vindico, ut aliis non negem. Sit sane, potest enim esse, sit honesta, sit sancta omnium intentio; esse autem occultissime profundissimeque rei humane conscientie iudex nolim. . . . tantum ut vitetur obscentitas, et que in imis esse solent sordes—id enim omnibus est necesse, qui quolibet in genere vitam agere procul ab infamia decreverunt. Sic obscena vitare debitum, in altum niti virtus est, pervenire felicitas." Zeitlin, 139.

not knowing that they do not know, they make no effort to know. The result is that they do not know to what end they are alive. How then should they love life when they do not know what it is good for?"[58] A consequence of this sad condition is indifference to salvation. Petrarch seems here to be elaborating a theory that those who are happy on earth will receive a heavenly reward while those who suffer, the vast majority, because of their indifference to their spiritual well-being, will founder and be condemned.[59]

The lack of any sense of direction or aim in life leads men to instability and changeability of mood, fickleness and lack of seriousness. Petrarch sees this condition of anomie, volatility, and rootlessness as leading to the adoption of forms of pseudostability and pseudoauthority. While he too flirted briefly with the notion that Cola di Rienzo might restore pristine Roman morality, and while he was the friend and beneficiary of many rulers, he did not consistently adhere to this most dangerous substitute for real security, attachment to a despot who promises to solve all one's problems. The chief danger Petrarch saw was not economic or political but psychological and moral. It lay in the tendency toward competitive imitation and adherence to swiftly changing fads and fashions.

> For though a man's nature may have vices enough of its own, most evils arise from a spirit of emulation and a hankering to imitate. And what imitator has ever been content with limiting himself to the error of his guide? We are anxious to excel and be conspicuous

58. *Prose*, 380–82; Zeitlin, 168–69.
59. *Prose*, 384–86: "Ita pars magna mortalium, seu volens, seu coacte, beluarum moribus procurva, in terram et corpori obsequens, animi negligens, sine virtutis illecebra, sine ulla notitia suimet spiritum trahit inglorium atque anxium; . . . hinc illa inquietudo animi qua nil peius patitur mortalis homo dum vivit. . . . Quomodo enim inter multos conveniat, cum secum quisque dissideat usque adeo?" Zeitlin, 171–72.

and to leave in our rear those whom at the start we followed.[60]

Imitation of this sort was the psychological counterpart
of the general social competitiveness of urban life. But it in
turn reinforced the competitive pattern. The individual,
detached from any center of activity within himself, became a passive participant in a circular social mechanism
controlled by forces outside and superior to himself.
Petrarch grasped the essentially alienating quality, the
simultaneous destruction of self and avoidance of self,
involved in emulation.

> There is no limit to their changes because there is no
> principle in imitation. Everything alien pleases them
> and anything of their own displeases them. They
> would rather be anything but what they are. In this
> feeling they would be justified if it arose from a serious
> consideration of their conditions instead of mere
> volatility.[61]

He leads this desire to escape back to the lack of self, "For
it is ignorance of our aim that produces all this evil,
whether it is peculiar to ourselves or common to all people,
the misguided know not what they do, therefore whatever
they do turns to disgust as soon as they have begun it."[62]
The disgust provoked by this kind of a life leads to a
despair with life itself, and to intermittent death wishes:
"With such eagerness do they urge on the flight of time as
must surely be the cause of death to many of them who,
always worrying over the future and bitterly hating the

---

60. *Prose*, 386; Zeitlin, 172.
61. *Prose*, 388–90: "Nullus itaque mutandi, quia nullus imitandi modus:
cunta illis aliena placent, sua omnia displicent, quidlibet esse malint quam
quod sunt." Zeitlin, 174.
62. *Prose*, 394; Zeitlin, 178.

present, are provoked to summon death through weariness
of living."[63] This passage reveals part of the psychology
underlying the morbid feelings that perhaps inspired Petrarch's recommendation of a meditation on death—the
terrible reality that alone could vie with the distracting
reality of competitive social life. The desire for death out
of weariness of life is an additional incentive to hope for a
life free from care in a heavenly afterworld, but such hope
can never be kindled except out of the concentration of
psychic energy in deep contemplation.

Petrarch is aware of this lack of any sense of command
over life as a reason why men have not wanted to exist:
they have not been able to endure the instability and alien
character of competitive social conditions. He is also
describing in this pessimistic view of urban life the same
condition of *acedia* he diagnosed in himself in the *Secretum*, but here it is applied to the *vulgus*. Petrarch held,
moreover, that these conditions cannot be changed. They
are endemic to cities, from which only the few may withdraw.[64] And he was troubled by the fact that not all men
could flee the city for a life of solitude. He asks himself
what would happen if they did and concludes that "we
should have to return forthwith to the places from which
the restless populace, father of all weariness, had departed."
There is no real possibility of this, however, since his doctrine is meant for the "happy few."[65] The rest of mankind
will have to be abandoned to their fate—to the miseries of
a life that they cannot call their own, and to future sufferings in hell. He and his companions can look forward to a
happier fate: "Let us send our souls before us to heaven;
when the time comes (which the philosophers did not

63. *Prose*, 396; Zeitlin, 178.
64. *Prose*, 402–04; Zeitlin, 184.
65. *Prose*, 580; Zeitlin, 310.

hope for) we shall follow with our bodies."[66] Solitude is a
heaven on earth reserved for those few individualists who
put their own salvation before that of others and live the
dream life of perpetual vacation in their country retreats.
Certainly Petrarch had not saved himself and his contemporaries from anything. His accomplishment, however, was
to give an amazingly fresh and penetrating analysis of the
effect on men of the new urban order which alienates
them from their creative capacities, their truest means of
human expression and self-development. He had also made
a truly modern distinction between a work that is a necessity and not our own, and a leisure that is our only freedom. "Leisure or freedom from responsibilities, call it
what you will, is the source of literature and the arts...."[67]
Further, he signaled the beginning of a shift in religion
from public communal expression to a private relationship
with the deity, and he exposed that fatal separation between what men did in public and what they privately
thought. Out of the traditional "double consciousness"
not only a twofold truth but a twofold ethic was emerging.
In one sphere of life (the external, public, social) men act
according to certain necessary conventions or compulsions.
There is no freedom there, and the best advice is to "submit patiently to circumstances." In the other sphere (the
internal, private, spiritual and moral) men have power and
freedom to change their feelings as they please, to accept
divine grace when proffered or spurn it.

   In fact, Petrarch's twofold "ethic" is not an ethic at all,
insofar as an ethic involves other men and action. It is
rather a roundabout way of yielding to the force of society
and also a way of protecting oneself from a complete sub-
mersion of the personality by a retreat to the inner world

66. *Prose*, 586; Zeitlin, 314.
67. *Prose*, 360; Zeitlin, 152.

of imagination. It is a social relationship confined to man
and his conscience, or to man and his God. Petrarch antici-
pates the Puritan's lonely struggle with his conscience by
three centuries. He quotes St. Paul's dictum that "none of
us liveth to himself and no man dieth to himself, for
whether we live, we live unto the Lord, and whether we
die, we die unto the Lord."[68] From this Petrarch concludes,
"And so you must live and die as if you lived and died
unto the Lord and to no other."[69] Yet he lacked the Puritan's zeal to make his actions conform to his religion. As
he admitted in his dialogue with Augustinus, he cannot
really avoid working for future fame and present reputation; thus his withdrawal amounted to a periodic, rather
than a perpetual, vacation.

The merit of Petrarch's analysis lies in his social and
psychological insights. He of course cannot explain why
the attitudes he described developed in the city. Nevertheless, he had encountered them in life as well as in the pages
of Seneca. His description of the aimlessness, the absence
of interest in anything beyond immediate gratification, the
inner despair, the imitativeness, the envy and resentment—
in short, the depersonalization and estrangement of city
life—brought to light a central feature of the modern moral
dilemma and its psychological accompaniments.

In both the *Secretum* and the *De vita solitaria* there is a
moral and religious confrontation between the kind of
man who is helplessly tossed about by his shallow emotional reactions to a fragmented urban social experience
and the man who has discovered a consistent course,
guided by consciously assumed moral values, and has
found inner peace in his hope of salvation. Both works
convey the same message through different means. The

68. Romans, 14:8.
69. *Prose*, 356; Zeitlin, 150.

imaginary debate between Augustinus and Franciscus brings back a beloved church father and saint to admonish and try to instill wisdom into the wayward personification of the author. In the *De vita solitaria* the contrast is between all those in human history who have sought peace in a life of solitude and those who have become the aimless, amoral victims of the chaotic necessities and fashions of urban life. Petrarch envisioned himself in the *Secretum* as avidly struggling to attain deep knowledge and strength of will while continuing to be drawn toward the destructive goals of worldly achievement. In the *De vita solitaria* he conceived of a possible compromise, a life within society that was morally directed, in which piety may be attained and the path to holiness entered. Thus in both works he wavered between his dramatic sense of an irreconcilable opposition between the two extremes and his more hopeful readiness to concede that some more temperate middle course was both possible and desirable.

Petrarch's *De otio religioso*, begun in 1347, should be seen as a companion work to the *Secretum* and *De vita solitaria*.[70] Here the manifest subject is the lives of the Carthusian monks in the same chapter house as his brother Gerardo—men who presumably have received the divine call and might be supposed by their constant meditations and devotions to have attained the holiness he was seeking. What emerges, however, is Petrarch's assumption that men who have become monks continue to experience the same conflicts of affect, imagination, and will and the continuous crises of purpose that afflict Christians living in the world. The only difference is that the circumstance of

70. Originally *De otio religiosorum*, it was later retitled *De otio religioso* to emphasize its parallelism to *De vita solitaria*, conceived as *De otio litteraria*. (Full reference in List of Works Cited.) See introduction by Martellotti, x–xv, on the versions and variants. See also *Prose*, 1168–69. For Petrarch's allusion to the parallelism of the two works, see *De otio*, 6, lines 28–29.

their cloistered lives makes their temptation imaginary and spiritual and possibly makes their torments more acute. In addition, Petrarch makes the work a review of his own career, of his turn from reading secular and pagan poetry to the Scriptures, of his discovery of the heroes of sacred as well as secular history, of his defense of pagan philosophy and his use of it to address the religious as he now uses the Scriptures to address his lay public. This work is also a clarification of his position on grace and free will, which he had left in a kind of limbo in the two previous works, skirting but never directly addressing it.

Petrarch's critical problem was to reconcile his constant urging toward personal moral autonomy, requiring many acts of free will for the attainment of virtue, with the need to assert and firmly establish the doctrine of grace. Could a man make the psychological and moral turn from anomie to autonomy unassisted by the divine mercy? The condition of Franciscus, of the *vulgus*, and of the *acedia*-burdened monk was one of deep moral and religious despair. Present in this deep *melancholia* were a self-hatred and total helplessness.

In the *Secretum* Franciscus could not heal his soul even with the deepest meditation because his will was both insufficient and divided. When Petrarch discusses St. Augustine's own experience of conversion under the fig tree, he has Franciscus acknowledge the obvious miracle of grace that transpired. Yet throughout the dialogues Franciscus insists he lacks the power, despite his willingness, to overcome his sinfulness. A similar sense of the inevitability of sinfulness pervades *The Life of Solitude*, though there are references to divine assistance. While addressing the monks in the *De otio religioso*, Petrarch is at last explicit. The monks' despair and *acedia* is the work of Satan, confusing and misleading their minds:

He will not dare to assert that anything is impossible to God lest by such open perfidy he rip away confidence in himself. What thence? He can do all; he wishes besides to give all goods to mankind; we however are unfit and unworthy to receive the divine gifts. And this meditation actually often disturbs the souls of many: God indeed is the best; I, moreover, the worst; what proportion is there in such great contrariety? I know not only by the authority of our writers but by Platonic assertion also how far removed envy is from that best one, and on the contrary I know how tightly iniquity is bound to me. Moreover what does it matter that He is ready to benefit when I am unworthy to be treated well? I confess the mercy of God is infinite, but I profess that I am not fit for it, and as much as it is greater, so much narrower, indeed, is my mind, filled with vices. Nothing is impossible to God; in me there is total impossibility of rising, buried as I am in such a great heap of sins. He is potent to save; I am unable to be saved. For however great the clemency of God, certainly it does not exclude justice, and mercy as immense as you wish must be reduced to the measure of my miseries; for no actions of agents are operative with regard to an incapable recipient, as pleases the natural philosophers; and although a weak spark may ignite a dry reed, the force of water extinguishes a great flame.[71]

Thus far this passage supports the posture of helplessness projected by Franciscus in the *Secretum* and reiterated in the *De vita solitaria*. But out of man's weakness and agony comes his hope for the aid of grace. Quoting Galatians 5:17—"For the flesh lusteth against the spirit and the spirit

71. *De otio*, 24–25; *Image*, 29, 334. My earlier discussions of the *De otio* are in *Image*, 28–47, 654–62.

against the flesh: and these are contrary one to another"—
and Romans 7:24—"O wretched man that I am, who shall
deliver me from the body of this death?"—Petrarch says:

> And resuming hope solely through the mercy of God,
> he should reply to himself: "I thank God through
> Jesus Christ our Lord"; to that one who alone is able
> to succor in this internal and domestic battle it must
> be cried out; he must be humbly beseeched that he
> should liberate us from the body of this death, whence
> the merit of man does not liberate but the grace of
> God alone [*unde meritum hominis non liberat sed
> gratia Dei solius*], to whom nothing I do not say is
> impossible, but not even difficult.[72]

Identifying at last with St. Paul rather than Cicero, Seneca,
and an Augustine whose Pauline theology of grace seems
curiously neglected, Petrarch affirms the only possible, and
orthodox, position that could be taken when the tension
between "spirit" and "flesh" was irreconcilable.

The emphasis on will, however, was powerful throughout
Petrarch's works. Grace was brought closer by continuous
and earnest striving to become virtuous. Virtue, as he says
in the *De otio religioso*, was not enough, nor was it the
final goal. The message of the *Secretum* is that virtue is not
a matter of easy rational perception but the attainment of
a deep and continuous emotional experience that trans-
forms the will and the *desiderium* into one concentrated
on salvation alone. Yet even when this has been achieved,
the agony of spiritual conflict continues until the gift of
grace relieves. Nor was the will that took hermits of old
and modern poets into solitude sufficient, though the
solitude of the countryside, as the isolation of the monastery, provided at least a setting of peace where the distractions of the world were less intrusive. And for those who

72. *De otio*, 66–67; *Image*, 40–41, 340–41.

live in the world, hopeless as their lack of direction might seem, they keep the possibility of regaining at least something of the moral autonomy and will that made them human.[73]

Petrarch, writing in imitation of St. Augustine, St. Paul, Seneca, and Cicero, engaged in the kind of creative role playing that seems to have been his characteristic mode of philosophizing. In so doing, he recapitulated elements of an ancient double consciousness. He applied the notion of a structural ambiguity in human consciousness, drawn from these pagan and Christian thinkers, to the spiritual dilemmas of his own experience. The consequences were remarkable. In the *Secretum* Petrarch explored the self in a lay confessional context, displaying the tensions between the immediate obligations of a poetic and professional career and the fascination of a more eschatological vision of death, damnation, and salvation. In the *De vita solitaria* he explored the relevance of the eremitic impulse, again in a lay and poetic context, contrasting the psychic and moral disintegration experienced in urban competitiveness with the imagined idyllic existence of the recluse living in literary or religious withdrawal. In the *De otio religioso* he compared the inner religious and psychic conflicts of the monk with his own development as lay poet and historian. Out of these literary and spiritual experiments, projecting a double consciousness of himself and his society, Petrarch attained an exceptional depth of psychological insight and an astonishingly realistic grasp of the social distempers of the late medieval urban world.

---

73. It was within the sphere of the pious layman (but also of the religious and the cleric who, though they might have taken their final vows or achieved ordination, nevertheless remained linked to "everyman" through their spiritual conflicts) that Petrarch began in these works initially written in the 'forties to project his more activist vision of the human arts of poetry and rhetoric as serving the moral and religious salvation of mankind.

4

Theologia Poetica and *Theologia Rhetorica* in Petrarch's *Invectives*

The medieval and Renaissance conception of *theologia poetica* was set forth by E. R. Curtius in his great work, *European Literature and the Latin Middle Ages*. Curtius saw the defense of poetry and the reassertion of *theologia poetica* in the Renaissance as both a resistance to the puritanical vigilance of those members of religious orders, usually Dominicans, who wished to suppress the joyful emulation of classical literary eroticism and as an effort to combat the downgrading of the liberal arts that had accompanied the triumph of scholastic theology.[1] There may also be seen in early Renaissance *theologia poetica* a positive assertion of the new vision of culture that culminated in the philosophic synthesis of Platonism and Christianity at the hands of Ficino and other Renaissance Platonists.[2] Petrarch, who was a Platonist only in aspiration, proposed that poetic theology and rhetoric, rather than philosophy were the intellectual instruments and disciplines best fitted for the pursuit of the Christian goal of salvation and the cure of souls. This chapter will examine two of his most forceful assertions of this new outlook.[3]

1. *European Literature*, chap. 12, "Poetry and Theology," 214-27, and especially 218-19, 226-27.
2. *Image*, chap. 15, "From *Theologia Poetica* to *Theologia Platonica*," 683-721.
3. The discussion will not try to relate the poetic and rhetorical Christian culture of the Renaissance to its many medieval precedents, at least from Augustine's *De doctrina Christiana* to the prescholastic culture of the twelfth

Petrarch in these polemics was also reaffirming the more traditional poetic and rhetorical nature of culture against the background of the triumphant scholasticism of both the theological faculty and the arts, where studies of dialectic and natural philosophy prevailed. His opposition is overtly to the latter in the two polemics *Invective contra medicum* and *De sui ipsius et multorum ignorantia* (*Invectives against a Physician* and *On His Own Ignorance and That of Many Others*).[4] But in his silence concerning scholastic theology, Petrarch abstains equally from praise and from blame. He attacks natural philosophy, it seems likely, because it was a more inviting target from a Christian moralist point of view (and not because it was the dominant branch of scholasticism in Italy). The combination of medicine and Greek natural philosophy, which was imitative of the Arabic culture from which its main textual sources were derived, left Italian natural philosophy especially open to Petrarch's jibes, although Averroës was as much an influence in the theological schools as in the arts.

Characteristically, Petrarch seized upon a specific occasion to deliver a general statement of his views, perhaps to gain that quality of immediacy so dear to him as well as contextual relevance. And yet he often contrived or even invented what he meant to seem spontaneous and sincere, so a suspicion of ambiguity about his motive in writing is aroused by nearly all of his works. Thus the *Invectives*

---

century. It assumes what is obvious, that the originality of statements made in a polemical context is not to be sought in literalness of statement but in relation to the larger context. In the history of culture nothing is truly original, but nothing is ever the same.

4. See List of Works Cited for full references. Valuable critical notes by Ricci on *Contra med.* are in *Prose*, 1171–72. *De ignor.* is also partially edited by Ricci in *Prose*, 710–67, using codices Vat. lat. 3359 and Hamilton 493. The Capelli edition uses only Hamilton 493.

against a Physician were prompted by a real event, the
illness of Clement VI in 1352. Petrarch sent Clement a
letter warning against his physicians, citing the harsh con-
demnations of doctors by Pliny, suggesting they counted
more on misplaced rhetoric than on medical skill in their
treatments, and that those who did so should be avoided as
assassins and poisoners. The pope should trust himself to a
single physician known for his science and his faith.[5]

Of the strength of his distrust and hostility to physicians
there can be little doubt, as this letter makes amply clear.
It cannot be known whether he anticipated the prompt
and angry reply he received from an anonymous member
of the medical profession, but he certainly seized the
occasion to amplify his position and extend it to a broad
cultural confrontation. This first answer to the physician
in spring 1352 was followed by another medical letter and
Petrarch's longer reply of 1353. In 1355 he combined his
statements, reworked and enlarged, into the four-book
Invectives. One may suspect that he provoked the occasion
to air his views, but this cannot be with certainty known.[6]

The *Invectives* are a brilliant polemical statement well
worth literary study of their rhetoric. Spurred by the in-
tensity of his contempt and the susceptibility to satire to
which medicine lies prey even today, Petrarch's attacks at
times become savage. One of the many examples will suf-
fice.

> I pray you do your mechanical acts; cure if you can; if
> not, kill! and demand your fee when you kill. What, by
> the blindness of mankind, is permitted to no emperor
> or king, is granted to you alone: to be the lord of life
> and of death, as you boast. Use your ghastly privilege,
> for you have delivered your brain to the best and

5. *Rer. fam.*, 5.19.
6. Cf. Ricci's account, *Prose*, 1171–72.

safest art. Whoever walks away owes his life to you; whoever dies, you owe him for nothing but experience; death is the fault of nature, or of the sick man: life is your gift. Socrates rightly said, when he heard of a man who had become a doctor after a career as a painter: "Let him be careful, for he has deserted an art which openly displays its defects for one whose errors the earth hides."[7]

Petrarch initially replies to the doctor's first counter-offensive and seeks to make clear what he did and did not say in his letter to the pope and to meet the doctor's claim that medicine is superior to the liberal arts, especially to rhetoric and poetry. It is a sacrilege, says Petrarch, to subject rhetoric to medicine, the lady to her maid, a liberal art to a mechanical. True, in our own age the vilest men rule over the finest, and so you think the arts should also be dragged under this kind of tyranny. The whim of fortune may make the Neros and Caligulas rulers, cause the Dionysiuses and Phalarises to flourish while a Cato wanders among Lybian plagues, a Regulus dies in prison, a Scipio in exile. "Fortune does all these things and similar ones in her accustomed way, playing as much as she wishes. But she cannot subject rhetoric to medicine, as she has no power beyond her own boundaries."[8]

That as a mechanical art medicine is useful to mankind, Petrarch does not deny. But it is like navigation and agriculture in that respect, not a liberal art or the mistress of rhetoric.[9] He expects that his opponent might even make

7. *Contra med.*, 29.
8. Ibid., 29–30.
9. Indeed, Petrarch suggests that the similarity of their social functions might make rhetoric the handmaiden of navigation, offering a possible economic interpretation of the rise of Renaissance rhetoric. Cf. ibid., 30. Ricci's footnote refers to Hugh of St. Victor, *Didascal.*, 2.24, and Uguccione da Pisa, *Magn. Der.*, s.v. *mercator*.

grammar subject to weaving and dialectic subject to arms making.[10] Petrarch wishes to think of his own humanistic arts of poetry and rhetoric as higher instruments devoted to the cure of souls.

In his *Secretum*, originally written a decade earlier but still being revised at this time, Petrarch first voices his conviction that his purpose as a writer might lie in offering cures for his contemporaries' spiritual maladies. Through Augustinus Petrarch assumes the role of spiritual doctor.[11] Augustinus tells Franciscus,

> Whenever in reading you come across salutary statements which, you feel, will arouse or quiet your soul, do not trust these to the powers of your mind but hide them in the depths of your memory and by much study make them familiar to yourself, so that, what experienced doctors are accustomed to do, in whatever place or time some urgent illness arises, you will have remedies written, as it were, in your soul. For there are certain passions in human souls in which, just as in bodies, delay is fatal, so that whoever removes the cure takes away the hope of recovery.[12]

Undoubtedly Petrarch felt a profound sense of rivalry with the physicians, which at this point in his career urged him into polemics against them. "You wish to speak on

10. There is a certain analogical appropriateness in these comparisons, which Petrarch takes from the medieval sources of his discussion of Mercury — Hugh of St. Victor and Uguccione of Pisa.

11. Franciscus's sins and conflicts are regarded as diseases of the soul to which Augustinus applies spiritual remedies. Tateo has argued (*Dialogo interiore*, 23–26) that Petrarch is using Franciscus as a vivid public example in a work meant as much for the edification of others as for the exploration of his own problems.

12. *Secr.,* in *Prose,* 122. Not long after he had written *Contra med.* he was writing his *De remediis,* in which he proposed cures in the name of *Ratio* for all sorts of psychic disorders resulting from excessive emotional reactions to specific types of good and bad fortune; see chapter 5.

any subject, forgetting your own profession, which is to contemplate urine and what shame keeps me from mentioning, but you are not ashamed to insult those whose responsibility is the cure of souls and the virtues."[13] Replying to the doctor's citation of Boethius that whorelike dramatic poets should be kept far away from the cure of the sick, Petrarch cites Boethius as saying, "Leave him to the true muses to be cured and made well." "These are the muses by whom, if any survive today, the poets are glorified and trusted, whose task, they teach, is not to afflict sick bodies but to succor sick souls."[14] It is interesting that in this discussion of two types of lay therapy no mention is made of the pastoral role of the clergy in the "cure of souls." However, the emphasis of the *Invectives* is to assert poetry (aided by rhetoric) as a source of philosophical and theological truth, and to argue the superiority of the psychotherapy of the liberal arts over the physician's bodily medicine.

Petrarch approaches this *theologia poetica* in book 2, which is primarily concerned with refuting the doctor's claim to be a philosopher as well as a master of rhetoric. True philosophy should be that which poetry conceals, rather than the dialectic the physician studies. The doctor asserts that Petrarch lacks logic, and Petrarch replies that logic includes grammar and rhetoric, which he rightly possesses, not just dialectic.[15] Petrarch has learned from the philosophers that none of the liberal arts is to be entirely honored. Though it is laudable to have learned them, it is childish to grow old clinging to them. They are means to something higher, not ends.[16]

---

13. *Contra med.*, 34–35.

14. Boethius, *De cons. phil.*, 1.1; *Contra med.*, 35-36.

15. *Contra med.*, 51.

16. Ibid., 52. Petrarch mocks the physician: "Tibi nobiliorem terminum non habenti, terminus quicquid occurrit. In summo te felicitatis gradu situm reris,

It was necessary for Petrarch to subordinate dialectic in order to set forth his conception of the role of the arts. Just as the thirteenth-century scholastics, and notably St. Thomas, considered the liberal arts preparatory subjects for the higher studies of philosophy and theology, so also does Petrarch. He would, however, substitute poetry as the true medium for philosophy and theology rather than the syllogistic demonstrations of dialectic used by the scholastics. In the prescholastic humanist tradition, both the late classical and the medieval Christian, poetry had also been considered the culmination of literary studies, for it dealt with divine matters. For Petrarch, moreover, it was important to assert that the elevation of dialectic to the basic methodological discipline and as an end in itself, as he argued his opponent was doing, led straight to atheism and heresy. In part this was a way to answer the charge that the poets were pagan and lascivious. Petrarch is at least as violent in his attack against dialectic as the zealots were in their condemnation of the poets. However, his attack was also a serious assertion that humanism was more compatible with Christianity than scholasticism and natural science.

Petrarch berates the doctor,

> Then, as a fool, you will say in your heart, "There is no God, nor is there anything higher toward which to aspire. For what do we know? Plato and Aristotle, great men, quarrelled over the world, the soul, ideas; Democritus made innumerable worlds; Epicurus held there was no god and the soul was mortal; Pythagoras placed the soul in a circuit; some confine it to its own body; some scatter it into the bodies of the living; some return it to heaven; some drive it into exile

---

quotiens unum forte fragilem sillogismum, et nichil ex nichil concludentem, multa cerebri vertigine tot insomni nocte texueris."

around the world; some plant it in the lower regions; some deny its existence; some think each soul created by itself; some think all souls are created together; there was also another one who more wonderfully dared to say a certain thing—our leader, Averroës, who attained to the unity of the intellect."[17]

He adds that no one but Averroës ever defamed Christ; no one spoke of Christ except with the greatest reverence, not even Mohammed, the prince of our greatest enemies. "Him [Averroës] you worship, him you love, him you follow after for no other reason except that you oppose and hate Christ the living Truth. And since you do not dare to blaspheme publicly Him whom the world adores, you adore his enemy [Averroës], a bit less of a sacrilege and blasphemy."

Returning to the doctor's trust in dialectic, Petrarch charges that he fights against simple Catholics armed with syllogisms—possibly Petrarch's real complaint against dialectical theology. The dialectician, however, is less likely to prove his opponent to be an ass than himself, as he grows old with his dialectic. "What greater stupidity than as an old man to be engaged for entire days on puerile things, and while you arrive home grey, to know nothing and not to dismiss these ineptitudes before unforeseen death suddenly concludes the matter for you while you are meditating on your little conclusions" (*conclusiunculas*).[18]

Petrarch contrasts with this the good end for a man, the meditation on death that he holds should be the true goal of philosophy. "This description of philosophy, although discovered by the pagans, nevertheless is properly that of Christians in whom both contempt of this life, as well as

17. Ibid., Does Petrarch anticipate the immortality debates of the sixteenth century here?

18. Ibid., 52–53.

eternal hope and the desire for dissolution ought to be."[19]
As in the *Secretum*, he makes meditation on death's great
reality the means by which the mind and soul are turned
toward a deeper consciousness than that which worldly
experience distractingly generates. True philosophy is
concerned with the reintegration and salvation of souls
in a clearly classical and Christian synthesis. Petrarch
again reconciles the two traditions as he had done in the
Secretum, where he caused Augustinus the Christian saint
and his father confessor to speak as a Stoic sage.

As he had also done in the *Secretum*, Petrarch rails
against the diversion of words from realities in this attack
on dialectical philosophy: "Listen to me, windy sophist—
forbear, noble logician, forbear if I call you a 'sophist';
reality itself drives me to do so, for where I see reality I
have no trust in contrary words; bring on your crooked
enthymeme, move up your *eculeum* [hobbyhorse]; you
may force me to concede, you will never drive me to
assent."[20]

After calling his opponent an *upupa*, or hoopoe bird,
not a philosopher, Petrarch presents his famous defense of
poetry as the key to divine insight. He thereby reverses,
in his own conception of a double consciousness, Plato's
famous opposition of dialectic to poetry as the key to
truth and reality. Petrarch's argument in book 3 is intri-
cate, and it is easy to become lost in the labyrinth of his
polemics. He wants to assert that medicine is not a branch
of philosophy or, by virtue of dialectic, a liberal art. It
is not a liberal but a mechanical art, and the dregs of the
mechanical arts at that, being the sixth of seven—the
seventh being the theatrical arts. At the same time, he
wants to reduce dialectical philosophy to the level of the

19. Ibid., 53–54.
20. Ibid., 54.

preparatory liberal arts and to elevate poetry (which had no place in the liberal arts though it was later made one of the *studia humanitatis*) to the superior position occupied by philosophy and theology. Poetry, with its hidden philosophy and theology, rather than scholastic philosophy and theology, should be the *maximus inter magnos*.

The coincidence of these invectives in time and subject matter with the denunciation of dialectic at the end of book 1 of *Le familiari* raises the question of the extent to which the text against physicians is also contrived. In any case, following the presumed arguments of his opponent, Petrarch next defends poets against the charge that they are opposed to the true faith. How could they be if the greatest Latin fathers all constantly cite the pagan Latin poets in their works? "On the contrary, almost none of the heretics insert anything of the poets in their little works either due to ignorance or because there was nothing in them consonant with their errors." Though the ancient poets cite the names of the gods, this should be considered as owing to the condition of the times and the peoples rather than their own judgment. "The greatest of these poets have confessed in their works one, omnipotent, all-creating, all-ruling, creator of things, God."[21]

It was argued moreover that poets are useless and unnecessary. Under this heading Petrarch pursues a long argument, with several subparts, to prove that the more necessary an art the less its nobility. The reverse is also true, as he uses arguments traditionally employed in behalf of philosophy to prove the elevated position of poetry in the hierarchy of the arts. It is here that he cites Aristotle's

21. Cf. *Rer. fam.*, 1, letters 7 to 12 "Ad Thomam Messanensem," then dead. The old Sicilian dialectician seems to have been an invention. See especially letter 7, where islands, such as Sicily and Britain, are said to be favorable to dialectic. *Contra med.*, 58–59.

Metaphysics—"Indeed all the others are more necessary but none are more dignified." To this Petrarch adds his declaration that poetry is the greatest among the great.[22]

His opponent charges that "scientia" deals with firm and unchangeable matters while poetry, according to Aristotle, uses changeable words. Petrarch easily disposes of this. The doctor misunderstands Aristotle, for in both science and poetry "the words change, the things on which the sciences are founded remain."[23] He also misunderstands Boethius, who is again cited as driving out the tragic muses and retaining his own presumably philosophical ones, but these are in fact poets themselves: Euripides, Lucan, and others.

The essence of the argument is whether philosophy and poetry are compatible. Since Seneca and Solon wrote poetry and Aristotle expounded Homer and Cicero translated him, they are. Petrarch agrees that evil dramatic poets can be rejected in favor of the better epic ones—but there are also evil philosophers, such as Epicurus. Even the greatest philosophers must be criticized. St. Paul, the true philosopher of Christ, and St. Augustine are amply cited to this effect. Yet Augustine praised Plato, who wished the dramatic poets driven from the city but not the heroic poets. In all this, including the obvious distortion of Plato's meaning, Petrarch follows St. Augustine. His point is to claim acceptability for the religious ideas of the poets. Just as there are bad philosophers, so there are bad poets, but not all are bad, not even before the advent of Christ. He talks of Homer and Vergil, who dealt with virtue and human perfection, and points out that there are faults in any age. "Who, therefore, does not know, or who would deny that certain of the poets, just as of the philosophers,

22. *Contra med.*, 61. Aristotle, *Metaph.*, 983a. 10–11.
23. *Contra med.*, 61–63.

grew vain in their thoughts? Or who should wonder that before the Advent of the Truth some errors would be allowed, when after the Truth was known also certain great catholics so departed from it that truth was never so sharply opposed as it was by them?"[24]

Petrarch next turns to Christian poets, who he claims make a higher contribution to the understanding of the truth than the philosophers—whether in the guise of physicians or not.

> Moreover, if anyone who is a friend of Truth, without which nothing can be called true, for as Augustine said all truth is true from the Truth, if any such a one, therefore, aroused by pious feeling, strives for the beauty of Truth itself with the aid of the muses, and celebrates in a distinguished style either the life of Christ, or something else sacred, or even profane provided it is not forbidden, which certain of our writers did . . . , who do you think could do this better? Certainly not Hippocrates or one of your doctors. Thus by the nature of their art, and by their very rarity, poets are nobler than those who administer to our necessitites, for their very arts are gifts of divine providence.[25]

The final charge he must meet is that the poets are obscure. It is exactly here that he is able to fill out his notion of the theological content of poetry. It is claimed that their obscurity is owing to the envy of the gods, but it is rather owing to their innocence and their friendship with the divine. Who could envy these marvelous men? Indeed their style may seem more hidden to those who are unaccustomed to poetry, but to those of a more intent mind it is a stimulus and the occasion for a nobler exercise.

24. Ibid., 63–66.
25. Ibid., 66–67.

Are not philosophers also difficult and obscure? Even Aristotle and Plato could be clearer, and Heraclitus the obscure deserves his nick-name. He repeats St. Augustine's raptures over the obscurity of the Scriptures and the wonderful variety of insights this permits.

Petrarch subscribes to what Curtius calls "Biblical Poetics"[26] —the doctrine that the Bible itself is poetry because it has to be interpreted allegorically. This is a medieval commonplace, and one that no one endorsed more enthusiastically than St. Augustine. For Petrarch, if the Scriptures, addressed to all men, had a mystical meaning, then even more did the poets who wrote for the few. "Among the poets therefore a majesty and dignity of style is retained, nor is it envied by those who are able to understand but is sought for the purpose of sweet labor and simultaneous delight and memory. The things we perceive with difficulty are dearer to us."[27] Some readers are repelled by the hidden meanings and follow other roads. The poets are content to please the learned few. "Certainly then an author will be valued when a sweet meaning erupts from hidden ways. . . . Certainly that poetic envy of the gods, which you recall, is for a certain higher and more secret mystery than you think; nor is there only envy of the gods among the poets but frauds, wars, lusts."[28]

Behind this is another idea. The first theologians were poets, as philosophers testify and the authority of the saints confirms. Petrarch repeats this medieval misunderstanding of Aristotle's statement in the *Metaphysics*. He also quotes Augustine that Orpheus and the other *prisci poetae* did not succeed in arriving at their goal, since

26. *European Literature*, 40 ff. and passim.
27. *Contra med.*, 70.
28. Ibid., 71.

"perfect knowledge of the true God is not of human study but of heavenly grace."

> Nevertheless the purpose of these most studious men should be praised who were certainly more able by these means to approach the desired height of truth, so that they preceeded the philosophers in this so great and necessary investigation. . . . These most ardent investigators of truth arrived at least at that point where it was possible to arrive by human genius . . . . They attained to some sort of knowledge of the first cause and the one God."[29]

Moreover, Petrarch asserts, the ancient poets, because they showed the gods at war with each other, struggles in which one had to be the victor and another the vanquished, knew that they were not true gods, "and so not immortal, nor omnipotent, and consequently not even a god; therefore they saw there was one God and not many; but the vulgar were deceived."[30] If the pagan poets erred, the pagan philosophers did also, but the crime is of the times and individuals, not of the art.[31]

One must ask what Petrarch, as a poet, considered his relation to this theological function to be. In 1348 or 1349 he had written to his brother Gerardo expounding his own first Latin eclogue as a religious poem beneath the surface. He had prefaced this with an explanation of the religious

29. Ibid.
30. Ibid., 72. I certainly agree with Ronald Witt that Petrarch did not think the pagan poets possessed grace and knew Christian truth. What he does say is that like the ancient philosophers they discovered monotheism and general religious truth. It is unclear to me whether one can deny inspiration of a lesser sort to them, as Witt believes I should have done in *Image*, for some of their truths were not even thought to be known to the poets. See Witt's article, "Coluccio Salutati and the Conception of the *Poeta Theologus* in the Fourteenth Century," 542–44.
31. *Contra med.*, 73.

origin and nature of poetry, speaking a hidden meaning through an *alieniloquium* (or foreign speech). "When at one time rude men, but burning with that desire which is innate in man for knowing the truth and for discovering the divine, began to think that there was some higher power by which mortals are ruled, they considered that power worthy to be venerated by a more than human ceremony and in an awesome ritual." In addition to temples, priests, vessels, and vestments,

> it was decided to please the divinity with high-sounding words and to confer a sacred praise to the higher powers by a style of speaking that was far from anything vulgar and plebeian, and confined to metres in which charm is present and boredom avoided. It was certainly necessary to create this, not in a vulgar form, but in a certain new and exquisite and highly artful way. Because in the Greek language this is called poetic, those who used it were called poets.[32]

In the *Invectives*, after a similar exposition of *theologia poetica*, Petrarch returns the argument to himself, since poetry had been denounced because he was known as a poet.

> And not so much the danger to my own fame, nor the offense to my name, although heavy I admit, aroused

32. *Rer. fam.*, 10.4.3–5. The first eclogue, as Petrarch interprets it, tells the story of his own life and that of his brother, how he entered the safer monastic way to God while Francesco became a poet. Since no one had praised the heroic virtues of Scipio Africanus and his supposedly divine origin in beautiful verse, Petrarch undertook to do so. "O that it may be concluded with as happy an exit as highmindedly it was begun by the youth! Certainly there always was a great danger in delay of the counsel of safety, and how various and unpredictable are the accidents of the present life, which the last speech of Monicus [i.e., Gerardo, the *Monachus*] ordered to be examined, need not even be said." Cf. *Petrarch's Bucolicum Carmen*, translated and annotated by Thomas G. Bergin (New Haven and London: Yale University Press, 1974), pp. 2–15.

> me to make these sermons as zeal here for truth and
> the indignity of your loquacity inflamed me. . . . For I
> do not arrogate to myself the name of poet, which I
> know could not happen to certain great men even by
> much study; but if it happened perhaps a little more to
> me, I do not reject it and I do not deny that I once
> youthfully aspired to it. Nor is my present program of
> daily readings touched by your injuries. I can swear,
> out of calumny as they say, that I closed the books of
> the poets seven years ago, and thus, since then, I do
> not read them—not that I regretted what I had read
> but because now it seemed superfluous to read them.

Instead, he now reads the Scriptures. "If these infused true
faith into Victorinus when he was an old pagan, God
speaking through them and softening the hardest breast,
why should they not infuse into me, a Christian, a firm-
ness of true faith and works and love of a happier life?"[33]

Petrarch also lays the foundation for a lay Christian
rhetoric that will become the counterpart of his Biblical
spirituality. His opponent accuses him of writing sermons
for the public in these invectives. Indeed, Petrarch readily
asserts that he does not care what his enemy thinks of
what he is saying, only his readers. But then he backs
away slightly, though in fact he is sermonizing. "And so
you call my little books *homilies* as if a premeditated word
of infamy, but one which is known to have pleased most
holy as well as most learned men. . . . Homily is a word of
Greek origin which can be called in Latin 'a speech offered
to the people.' Certainly I in these writings address nothing
to the people but to your ignorance. If by any chance I
were able, I would not speak to wrench that out of you
but pride out of them."[34] Petrarch was turning more and

33. *Contra med.*, 73–74.
34. Ibid., 75.

more to rhetoric, which he wished to employ for moral and religious ends—toward what might be called *theologia rhetorica* in analogy to a similar conception and employment of poetry as *theologia poetica*.

He completes the third invective against the doctor by turning again to the claim that rhetoric is a servant or an auxiliary science to medicine. Petrarch is savage in his irony.

> For what need does a sick man have for a long oration, to whom every word is an annoyance, unless that he is helped to be in a good disposition and is cured by aid of the art, if it is possible? . . . There is one matter in which I may excuse this alien study of eloquence in you: if perchance you think that eloquence, I do not say supplements, but hides your defects and ignorance of medicine, and when you openly kill someone, you show that the blame is not yours but that of the sick man, or of the bystanders, or of nature; or if, moreover, in the case of death received at your hands you wish to console the survivors. For I confess there is need of orators and rhetoric in both these cases. To accuse, to excuse, to console, to irritate, to placate souls, to move to tears and to remove them, to light fires of anger and to extinguish them, to color facts, to avert infamy, to transfer blame, to arouse suspicions—these are the proper works of orators; I would not know them to be those of physicians.[35]

Finally Petrarch ironically opposes his own syllogism to his opponent's fallacies.

> Think and rethink your syllogisms; you will find them inane and vacant. . . . Would you, however, receive a

35. Ibid., 78.

solid and universal syllogism from one who is lacking in logic? Just as a rational soul, unless it loses its reason, rules over its own body, the body also serves it; so all arts invented on account of the soul rule over those invented on account of the body, and the latter therefore are the servants. Moreover it is established that the liberal arts have been invented on account of the soul, the mechanical arts on account of the body. Then conclude dialectically: therefore, rhetoric is servant to medicine. Physician, you have what you wished.[36]

Petrarch's major effort to discriminate wisely between philosophy and rhetoric, his *On His Own Ignorance and That of Many Others*, also deserves careful consideration. In *On His Own Ignorance*, Petrarch again seizes upon his response to a presumed insult to explore a more universal meaning. This tendency to make his own situation a metaphor for everyman's may be called a poetic mode of thinking.[37] He allows that "whoever calls me ignorant shares my opinion. Sorrowfully and tacitly I recognize my ignorance, when I consider how much I lack of what my mind in its craving for knowledge is sighing for."[38] What he does not overtly acknowledge is the Socratic model for this stance.

The great importance of this work, which seems to criticize Aristotle and praise Plato, is that Petrarch actually rejects philosophy in favor of rhetoric and rhetorical poetry. This is shown by his emphasis on the will. He will strive, Petrarch says, with all his energy to be a good man "and shall not tire until my last breath and my last sigh."[39] Addressing Seneca, who advised Lucilius to be content

---

36. Ibid., 79.
37. Cf. chapter 1, pp. 23-24 and n. 59. Cf. also Tateo, *Dialogo interiore.*
38. See List of Works Cited for full references. *De ignor.*, Nachod, 66. In some of the passages, I have modified his translation to make it more literal.
39. Ibid., 71.

with the title of a good man rather than a man of letters, Petrarch adds, "You once said elsewhere that I must have will-power to be good. If the will accomplishes this task it will be good; if it only makes a start, then desiring to be good is at least a part of being good."[40] Later comes his much quoted statement, "It is better to will the good than to know the truth." It is perhaps of no great importance that the word translated as "better" is *satius*, not *melius*, a perfectly legitimate translation, although one that may obscure the more subjective and pragmatic quality of *satius*—"it is more sufficient or more satisfying to will the good than to know the truth."[41]

Shortly before, Petrarch declared that Aristotle had failed to fulfill the promise made at the beginning of the *Ethics* that "we learn this part of philosophy not with the purpose of gaining knowledge but of becoming better."[42] Aristotle's purpose coincides with Petrarch's, but Aristotle does not succeed in transforming the will. Aristotle "teaches what virtue is," "but that text does not have the incitements and the shaping of words by which the mind is urged and inflamed to love of virtue and hatred of vice, or it has very little of them."[43] Aristotle's is a rhetorical, not a philosophical, failure. One finds the needed force to activate the will instead in Cicero and Seneca and Horace. "Everyone who is familiar with our Latin authors knows that they stamp and drive deep into the heart the sharpest and most ardent stings of speech by which the lazy are

40. Ibid. Cf. Seneca, *Epist.*, 88.38.
41. *De ignor.*, Nachod, 105, *Prose*, 748: "Satius est autem bonum velle quam verum nosse."
42. *Eth. Nic.*, 1.1.1094b23–1095a6.
43. *De ignor.*, Nachod, 103; *Prose*, 744: "Docet ille, non infitior, quid est virtus; at stimulos ac verborum faces, quibus ad amorem virtutis vitiique odium mens urgetur atque incenditur, lectio illa vel non habet, vel paucissimos habet." (My translation.)

startled, the ailing are kindled, the sleepy aroused, the sick healed, the prostrate raised, and those who stick to the ground lifted up to the highest thoughts and to virtuous desire."[44] One can contrast this with Petrarch's attack on the physician's misuse of rhetoric. Here pure rhetoric is employed for moral and Christian purposes, for the cure of souls, but it can be seen how he puts forth rhetoric as an alternate kind of theology to the learned philosophical theology of scholasticism.

Initially Petrarch reminds us that outside the teaching and aid of Christ no one can become wise, virtuous, or good.[45] The Scriptures, not the writers and poets of antiquity, are the true source of Christian inspiration. But the rhetorical authors can certainly help, because they teach how to stimulate virtue, which, while it is not itself the goal, leads to the goal. "It is through the virtues that the direct way leads to the place where it does lie." They are true moral philosophers because they "do not merely teach what virtue and vices are," the fault of Aristotle, but "sow in our hearts love of the best and eager desire for it." "It is safer to strive for a good and pious will than for a capable and clear intellect."[46] His famous declaration follows: "The first"—that is, to will the good—"is never without merit; the latter"—that is, to know the truth—"often even has guilt and offers no excuse for it. Therefore they widely err who spend their lives in learning to know virtue, not in acquiring it, in learning to know, not in loving God."[47]

44. *De ignor.*, Nachod, 144.
45. Ibid., 104–05.
46. Ibid., 105.
47. *Prose*, 748: "Illud enim merito nunquam caret; hoc sepe etiam culpa habet, excusationem non habet. Itaque longe errant qui in cognoscenda virtute non in adipiscenda, et multo maxime qui in cognoscendo, non amando Deo tempus ponunt."

The significance of this argument is that it denies the validity of a philosophic pursuit of knowledge of God. "In this life," Petrarch says, "it is impossible to know God in his fullness."[48] It would be worse not to know God at all, of course, for unknown things are not loved. But a simple and limited knowledge is sufficient—"to know God and virtue so far as to know that He is the most lucid, the most fragrant, the most delectable, the inexhaustible source of all that is good, from which, through which and in which we are as good as we are."[49]

Petrarch is arguing that rhetoric be given an almost exclusive role in bringing Christians to God and making them good. He speaks of "our own philosophers"[50]—meaning the Latin Cicero and Seneca—as preferable to the Greeks, but he employs them rhetorically for the task of transforming men's wills to goodness and love of God. Earlier in *On His Own Ignorance* Petrarch had written at length about Cicero's *De natura deorum*, trying to find the philosophy that he would have liked to find there. "Of all the writings of Cicero those from which I often received the most powerful inspiration are the three books . . . *On the Nature of the Gods.* . . . When I read these passages I often have compassion for his fate and grieve in silent sorrow that this man did not know the true God."[51] Petrarch reports all the pleasing things he finds in Cicero, particularly concerning the creation and divine providence. But in the end he concludes, "The ancients, and particularly Cicero, may pardon me if I say: this great man devoted much energy to compiling what, as it seems to me, ought not to have been written."[52] What is left is Latin rhetoric. Petrarch

48. *De ignor.*, Nachod, 105.
49. Ibid., 106.
50. Ibid.
51. Ibid., 79.
52. Ibid., 91.

rejects Greek philosophy, especially Aristotle, even though he treats him with great respect. He longs to know Plato but in the end recognizes that he cannot accept the Greek as he was not a Christian.

Petrarch endorses the primacy of the will and man's striving to be good. This doctrine developed within the Franciscan school of scholastic philosophy, particularly in Duns Scotus and in Bonaventura's emphasis on charity, and was widely taken up by the Augustinian Friars with whom Petrarch had intimate ties.[53] The primacy of the will does not eliminate scholastic theology, but it leads to the kind of covenantal, Scripture-based theology of the Ockhamists. This was a position at which the humanists also arrived, following Petrarch, based on an Augustinian and humanistic foundation. Another parallel with the Ockhamists that follows from his voluntarism is Petrarch's assertion that striving to be good is the equivalent of being good. This matches the famous principle of *facere quod in se est*—to do one's very best.[54]

Contemporary theology may have set the mood, but probably more determining for Petrarch was the doctrine of the will inherent in ancient rhetoric. Ancient rhetoric was a probable source of St. Augustine's voluntarism as well, and Augustine's doctrine of will paradoxically accompanies his emphatic soteriology of grace. Petrarch shared the view that man's salvation came by grace alone. And this belief he thought necessary to arouse his contemporaries from their sloth of despair and sense of moral incapacity. But the moralist's call with his homilies and his rhetoric is also not in vain. Grace comes only to those who are ready for it and welcome it, and for this a sense of

---

53. Cf. Ugo Mariani, *Il Petrarca e gli Agostiniani*.
54. Cf. H. A. Oberman, *Harvest,* 132 and 468. Cf. passages cited pp. 107-08 in notes 39 and 40, and pp. 60–61.

possessing some degree of moral autonomy was also essential.[55] In his later years Petrarch worked tirelessly to provide the literary means for arousing this sense of moral capacity.[56]

In the *Invective* and *On His Own Ignorance*, Petrarch lays forth his ideas concerning the nature and value of the different disciplines. Written as defenses, they turn into powerful assertions of a point of view that became paradigmatic for the entire early humanist movement—the assertion of the lay writer's vocation as a moral counselor, as a poetic and rhetorical theologian, as a guide to the perplexed. His call was to all those who felt deprived of a sense of self in the frantic scramble of daily affairs in the commercial, ecclesiastical, and political worlds of the mid and late Trecento. It was a call to them to recover their moral consciousness, and to contemplate their eternal destiny.

It may seem that by turning to morally and religiously directed rhetoric and poetry Petrarch reverted to the single consciousness of a Protagoras, one of the founders of the rhetorical tradition.[57] Petrarch sees the poet and preacher as inspired by Christian faith, using the literary arts to arouse the moral sense and faith of the dispirited and demoralized man. But Protagoras, too, claimed the capacity to make a man better but not wiser. The method and the stance are the same, but Petrarch as a Christian seems also to retain the counterconsciousness that Socrates was

55. See chapter 3, pp. 86–89, for Petrarch's discussion of grace and despair; *Image*, 28–41.

56. Especially on his *De remediis* (cf. *Prose*, 1170) which was completed in 1366 and circulated in 1367. The second invective discussed here, the *De ignor.* (cf. *Prose*, 1173–74) was provoked in 1366; its first and final versions were written in 1367. Another autograph, copied in June of 1370, was issued to the world in January 1371.

57. Plato's version of Protagoras's position in the *Theaetetus*, making him a representative of an experience-based consciousness, is discussed in chapter 2.

shown as seeking in Plato's *Theaetetus*. The adoption of *theologia poetica* and *theologia rhetorica* in the Renaissance seems emphatically to have also required a higher religious consciousness, however much it rested on the Protagorean premises. If the systematic theologian points out that the loose poetic and rhetorical assumptions of Petrarchan humanism lack any conception of the whole of the universe, he does not reckon with the potency of Petrarch's writings, or those of Coluccio Salutati, Lorenzo Valla, or Erasmus, all of whom followed Petrarch's initiative. The spread of the doctrine of the primacy of the will was necessarily a powerful stimulus to the rise of a poetic and rhetorical spirituality and to the decline of philosophical and metaphysical theology.

5

Estrangement and Personal Autonomy in Petrarch's *Remedies* and in Boccaccio's *Decameron*

The fourteenth century witnessed the beginning of a search for a new mode of reconciling heaven and earth, God and man. Both Petrarch and Boccaccio made major contributions to this search and these friends clearly recognized each other's efforts toward a solution of this problem. The search provoked an amazing range of attempted solutions from the late medieval and early Renaissance cultures of the fourteenth and fifteenth centuries through the seismic religious upheavals of the sixteenth and early seventeenth centuries. In the seventeenth century, Descartes' severing of the spiritual and the material, which solved the problem by rejecting the possibility of a solution, inspired the renewed attempts of Kant, Hegel, and the German idealists in the late eighteenth and the nineteenth centuries. Today, particularly in the Anglo-American cultural tradition, there is a scepticism toward the large and the metaphysical solution and a preference for breaking down the problem into the concrete, the personal, and the circumstantial. This attitude has created a receptivity toward the kinds of explorations made by the early humanists, particularly Petrarch and Boccaccio.

The fourteenth century lived in the shadow of the great intellectual and artistic achievements of the thirteenth. Though there was but one Dante, the many rivals of Thomas Aquinas composed their own great summas, and it seems to have been within the sacred walls and precincts of scholastic theology that the fourteenth-century revolt against absolutism first occurred. A generation or two ago, this period was seen as one of scepticism and decline sandwiched between two great ages of faith—the Gothic and the Lutheran. The present generation of scholars tends to see it neither as the beginning of a secularist overthrow of clerical piety, nor as the undermining by the sharp logic of Ockham's razor of untenable philosophical and theological preconceptions, nor as the eager embrace of ancient paganism by the humanist scholars and their friends. Modern scholars see instead lay piety, a fervent theological embracing of man's own spirituality, and the discovery of the sacral character of a Greek and Roman antiquity that prepared the way for the advent of Christ. Few humanists wished to leave Homer and Vergil to wander aimlessly in Limbo as Dante had felt compelled to do. It was not long until Erasmus would say, cautiously but sincerely, "Sancte Socrate, ora pro nobis."

The judgment, once universal, that nominalism was the primary characteristic of fourteenth-century theology should be modified, though not discarded. The term "nominalism" cannot be usefully abandoned, but a more significant signature of late medieval scholastic theology is what has been called "the dialectic of God's *potentia absoluta* and *potentia ordinata*"—God's absolute power and his ordered power. It seemed necessary to assume the deity's absolute power to act without being limited by feeble human perceptions and conceptions of the natural or the divine. To William of Ockham and to many other thinkers, this assumption freed the deity to create this world as it actually is without the necessity for man to conceive of it as conforming to preestablished metaphysical principles. God's ordered power, that is, his employment of his power in the act of creation, gave the world and human history, with all its seeming obscurities and contradictions, their form, just as man dimly perceived it either through science or revelation. The world or history need not be neat, or orderly, or rational, or logically necessary, but however the world appeared to human perception, it was full of contingency, since that was the world that happened to be created when God in His absolute power could have created anything or nothing. But at the same time man had to believe what God had revealed to him about the world and about his wishes for mankind and for its salvation. The positing of a divine absolutism and of the contingency of the created order did not result in the idea that this world was, as scholars had once seen it, separate from or opposed to the divine. What God had wrought was fully divine and contained within itself the potential for sanctification and salvation for man. Everything shown in Scripture or revealed to man by God through other means, in particular God's "Book of Nature," could be accepted as actual and divinely created. At the same time, a much stricter determination of the meaning of the divine Word in its many manifestations and a more rigid adherence to God's commandments seemed inescapable.[1]

Petrarch was a professed archenemy of scholastic thought. And yet, for all his efforts to find classical models for literature, history, philosophy, and especially for morality, he was very much a man striving to come to terms

---

1. There is therefore less need to be puzzled by the late medieval and early modern embrace of biblical literalism and natural empiricism. We must see the quest for scientific understanding as occurring within a religious context and not as an assertion of secularism and scepticism. For the contents of these first three paragraphs one might cite fifty items. *The Pursuit of Holiness* was only one of many recent attempts to confront the problems described; see my foreword for a summary. See also Oberman, "The Shape of Late Medieval Thought," and his "Fourteenth-Century Religious Thought," as well as William J. Courtenay, "Nominalism."

with his own times. His haunts were not only the caves and springs of the Vaucluse but the thriving cities of Avignon, Milan, and Venice. He visited some of the most powerful courts and rulers of Europe. His epic poem on the life and exploits of Scipio Africanus, the *Africa*, presented the virtues of this general and statesman alongside those of the Latin epic poet Ennius. Both are crowned on Rome's capitol, as Petrarch was later to be.[2]

Much of his writing seems, though, to turn away from the active life of the seeker of fame, whether ruler or poet. The ideal of withdrawal and of religious, literary, and philosophical contemplation is emphasized. Petrarch holds himself up as an example of the man who has heard the call to virtue and piety but cannot break the bonds of habit. Augustinus, Petrarch's fictional replica of St. Augustine in the *Secretum*, tells Franciscus, Petrarch's depiction of himself, that he has the power and the will to withdraw and meditate, and hence to reintegrate his scattered feelings in a concentrated contemplation of death and damnation that will lead him to eternal life. Yet Franciscus cannot do so.[3] Petrarch weighs the monastic path followed by his brother Gerardo, but he cannot follow it.[4] He seeks in his lay career to find a reconciliation between the virtues of the pagans, the ideal of worldly and artistic achievement, and salvation.[5]

---

2. Aldo S. Bernardo, *Petrarch and the "Africa"*; the entire volume deals with this event and its meaning. Cf. Petrarch's *Africa*, ed. Nicola Festa, and his *De viris illustribus*, ed. Martellotti, for his concern with the ancient man of action.

3. See chapter 3, pp. 59–65.

4. Cf. *Rer. fam.*, 10, *epist.* 3, 4, 5.

5. Although Petrarch held minor orders, recited some masses, and lived on benefices, as E. H. Wilkins has shown ("Petrarch's Ecclesiastical Career," chap. 1 of his *Studies*), he considered himself a man of the secular world, as he makes clear in the *Secretum* and the letters cited in note 4. Cf. *Image*, 41–50.

In his *Life of Solitude*, Petrarch seems to turn against the world toward the Stoic dualism he learned from Seneca and attributed to Augustinus in the *Secretum*. Here it is no longer Petrarch who is torn between conflicting desires and has lost his direction but the city dweller, both rich and poor. Petrarch would withdraw from the city and its hopeless crowd; yet he charts not only the delights of his rural retreat but also a course of life in the world characterized by virtue and piety. Through this he seeks a personal autonomy that can transcend the alienation suffered by the vulgar.[6] In his work on *Religious Withdrawal* addressed to Gerardo and his Carthusian brothers, Petrarch sees delight and peace and freedom from distraction in the monastery but also alienation. In the throes of monastic meditation there can come from within the self-destructive thought of the unconquerability of one's own sins, and from this a hopeless and reckless despair of salvation.[7] In his hypersensitivity he can visualize the monkish experience as resembling Luther's *Turmerlebnis*, from which one can be saved only by total dependence on grace. But for the man in the world, who is farther from the ultimate reckoning with his ineluctable sinfulness than the monk, it is enough to seek a life of conventional virtue. This is sufficient to restore to him the possession of his own soul. Thus in all of his works from the early *Africa* to the early 1350s, Petrarch, who was in so many ways a cultural elitist, is also deeply concerned with the *vulgus*—within himself, in the man in the street, and even in the monk and poet. For Petrarch the *vulgus* means lack of culture but also the lack of the discipline and morality that come from culture, knowledge of history, letters, philosophy, and the arts.

6. See chapter 3, pp. 76–79.
7. *De otio* as cited in chapter 3. Cf. *Image*, 28–41.

Petrarch always regarded himself as having a mission for his own times. Even when he seems to profess the most complete withdrawal from society he is trying to save souls—not only for the next world, but for the sake of a more decent and pious earthly existence. His strategy was indirect. He would either totally reform culture and education by turning to the classics as models, or he would offer the example of his own travails as a salutary lesson in the importance and difficulty of findings one's bearings.[8]

From the early 1350s until his death, Petrarch waged a more overt campaign of moral reform, though without turning totally away from his earlier literary-moral stance. Now it is to be rhetoric and not poetry that is the medium of his sermonizing. He must first, however, establish its greater relevance to theology and moral reform than the scholastics' dialectic. The latter is an elementary subject, and it cannot move men, so that its practitioners remain walled off from their fellows by their idiocy, whether one is alluding to the medieval or the modern meaning of the term. Poetry discovers and reveals divine truths even before the Advent; rhetoric transmits and persuades to conviction and action. Truth is not scientific; truth is psychological and fruitional, the vision that reconciles man to his divinely created universe and redeems him from his worst impulses.

Nowhere does Petrarch seem to attack scholastic theology as such. By attacking, instead, scholastic natural philosophy, he is concerned with its confusion with rhetoric and its misuse as a mode of psychotherapy by the physicians who are its practitioners. The poet and humanist, the rhetor, may legitimately cure souls, not the physician. If the natural philosopher limited himself to the theoretical investigation of nature through Aris-

8. Tateo, *Dialogo interiore*, argues this effectively.

totelian texts, Petrarch would not mind, but when he attempts to use them to theorize about divinity and to save souls he does mind. This was Petrarch's way, by implication, of attacking the scholastic and clerical saver of souls. He offers his own sermons instead, as he suggests he will do in the *Invectives against a Physician.* He never mentions the theologians or the pastor, but he is clearly offering his own pastoral theology in place of theirs.[9]

Petrarch's sermons and cures for souls are to be found in his letters and especially in his *De remediis utriusque fortunae—Remedies for Good and Bad Fortunes*—completed in 1366.[10] Until modern times, despite the popularity of his lyrics, this was Petrarch's most widely read work, and it remained popular until the mid-eighteenth century when the last printed edition of it was issued.[11] It was obviously very carefully attuned to the mentality of late medieval and early modern Europe. Nearly twenty years ago, Klaus Heitmann analyzed this work in his *Fortuna und Virtus.*[12] *Fortuna*, Heitmann found, was used in many ways by Petrarch, but in the end the word was a mode of speaking and not a concept in which he believed. All events ultimately came from God, all the accidents of fortune that befell an individual, the good and the bad. The good events generate passions of overoptimism and self-congratulation in their recipients—*Gaudium* and *Spes.* Bad events generate suffering and fear, or *Dolor*

9. See chapter 3 for analysis of *Contra med.*

10. Cf. the editorial note in *Prose*, 1170. There is no modern edition of *De remediis*; I have used *Opera omnia*, Basel, 1554, 1–256, and Twyne.

11. There were many manuscripts, and it was quickly translated into French and soon into Italian, German, English, Catalan, Spanish, and Czech. See, for the MSS, Nicholas Mann, "The Manuscripts of Petrarch's 'De remediis,' a Checklist"; for editions and translations, see W. Fiske, *Petrarch's Treatise De Remediis.*

12. What will be said in this chapter about the *De remediis* will be supplementary to Heitmann's study. His analysis was basically conceptual and formalistic, attempting to discover a systematic pattern of thought in the work but neglecting the manifest content.

and *Timor*. The first two are personified and matched against Reason or *Ratio* in the first book; *Dolor* and *Timor* oppose *Ratio* where bad fortunes are discussed in the second. But there is little discussion. *Gaudium* and *Spes* boast about or anticipate their good fortune in a series of reiterated sentences; *Dolor* bemoans her bad luck in similar fashion. *Ratio* does all the talking. In fact the work is a collection of little sermons, with a few longer ones, all by *Ratio*, alias Petrarch.

Fortuna does not play an extraordinary part in *De remediis*. Although there are calamities and sudden shifts toward prosperity, for the most part Petrarch is not talking about caprice and accident but of the ordinary course of life, of the ordinary range of events, and of the ordinary organization of society. His *Fortuna* is in fact human society and human history in its patterned and structured variety. It is encountered by the individual according to his changing place in the scheme as he passes through the course of a lifetime. These encounters, though not lacking in contingency and chance, are not, by and large, extraordinary.

Petrarch puts together several traditional organizational schemes. These tend to overlap, and he does not hesitate to introduce variations. Book 1 deals with the harmful effects of so-called prosperous fortune and their remedies. These supposedly good things that produce harmful effects begin with the "goods of the body"—flourishing years, bodily beauty, bodily health, health restored after illness, bodily strength, bodily swiftness (chaps. 1–6). Their source, though he doesn't mention it, is Aristotle's *Nicomachean Ethics*, which itself reports Hellenic conventional wisdom. This is followed, traditionally enough, with the goods or joys of the mind: wit, memory, eloquence (of special interest for the sharpness of the humanist's critique), virtue, reputation of virtue, wisdom, and religion (chaps. 7–13). Perhaps they should rather have been called goods of the soul. Next follows a long section of thirty-five chapters each dealing with a so-called external good, again Aristotle's category (14–48). What is actually contained here is a survey of all of the pleasures of the upper classes of his day. There follow four chapters on the treacherous pleasures of friendship (49–52).

Next Petrarch presents a series on riches (chaps. 53–64). Here he again offers a vivid image of contemporary life, dealing first with urban wealth: having plenty of money, finding a gold mine, finding treasure, usury; then with rural property and possessions—fruitful, well-tilled lands, pleasant green walks, flocks and herds of cattle, then, more exotic, elephants and camels, apes, peacocks, chickens, bees, pigeons, fishponds, cages of birds. Riches are the first of the conventional trio of wealth, honor, and power, but he comes to the others (91 and 92) after a double interruption. A long section on the false joys of marriage and family life (65–84) and a short collection of miscellaneous prosperities such as arriving in harbor, release from prison, and the peace of retirement precedes single chapters on power and glory (85–90). This is followed by social successes—benefits bestowed or magnanimity—followed by love from the people. This category is essentially political, and he pursues this theme at length, dwelling on the successes of war and politics, culminating with election to the papacy (93–107). Behind this seems to be the second book of Cicero's *On Duties*, which deals with the utilities and expediencies of public life. Finally there is a long summary chapter on happiness (108). But this is not all. Up to this point the dialogue has been between joy and reason. A second part to this first book follows, with hope replacing joy. Future or anticipated joy is as unreliable in its prophesied coming as present joys are unsubstantial (109–122).

The structure of book 2 on adverse fortunes is even more inconsistent and difficult to follow, although it is discernible. Starting with deformity, weakness, and disease of the body, it promises to match the order of book 1. But these troubles are connected with a section on disasters of birth—a bad country, a lowly family, bastardy, slavery (1-7). This leads into poverty and the financial troubles of both the poor man and the merchant, including business loss, standing surety, and loss of time (8-16). There follows a very long section on troubles arising from family life and personal relationships—friends, enemies, neighbors, servants, lords, and masters (17-53). Then comes a section on calamities such as shipwreck, fire, famine, and loss through being a victim of crimes (54-63). This leads into a long section on sufferings owing to political oppression and war (64-74). He next takes up old age and its ills, leading into the ills of the body and then the ills of the mind, apparently parallel to the categories of goods in the first book (75-104). Midway through the ills of the body comes chapter 93 on the misery of man, which is his famous counterstatement of the dignity of man, perhaps the first humanist treatise on this theme. It is sandwiched between the plague and the toothache.[13] The final ill of the soul is lack of virtue, matching the seeming virtue of book 1, and this leads naturally enough to a serial treatment of the seven deadly sins (105-111). Again he reverts to the body with agues, trances, pains of the gut, and a lengthy chapter on sundry pains and griefs of the whole body, which is a treatise on the capacity of rhetoric to cure (112-114). Finally, fear and sorrow turn to all sorts of deaths (115-132).

The partially concealed principle of organization is to run through a life course from birth to maturity to old

13. For a detailed discussion, see *Image*, 179-96.

age to death discussing all possible events, but this pro-
cedure is interrupted by different classifications as the
work progresses. This attempted reconstruction of the
content structure of the *Remedies* reveals both Petrarch's
categories of classification and the range of his interests
and knowledge of the historical world of man. It does not
follow the pattern of works on the complaints of the three
estates[14] but comes closer in content to classical moral
treatises, especially to Aristotle's and Cicero's, though the
allegorical format is medieval.

A more important theme revealed by Petrarch's method
is his total focus on the individual as an individual, tri-
umphing in his successes and grieving on his sorrows. The
individual faces the world and life in a state of alienation,
but he can rise above his alienation by achieving personal
autonomy. Alienation and autonomy are two sides of the
same coin; one does not exist without the other. Autonomy as an ideal is based on the negative ideal of alienation;
the fear of alienation derives from the desire for autonomy.

Petrarch's concept of man's position in the world aptly
illustrates Burckhardt's conception of Renaissance individualism;[15] indeed, it illustrates the whole modern moral
debate. Yet in a very genuine sense it is not modern at all
but medieval and Christian. In its origins it is antique. This
structure of human relations can be perceived in Plato's
conception of Socrates' pursuit of moral autonomy; it goes
to the heart of Aristotle's *Ethics* with its eudaemonistic
pursuit of individual happiness. It corresponds to the underlying assumptions of rhetoric that individuals pursue

14. Cf. Ruth Mohl, *The Three Estates in Medieval and Renaissance Literature.*
15. Cf. Burckhardt's remarks at the beginning of part II of *The Civilization
of the Renaissance in Italy*, "The Development of the Individual." But his
comments are scattered throughout the book. Cf. also part VI, chapter 1,
"Morality and Religion."

their happiness according to their circumstances, and the orator, knowing this, is then capable of reaching and moving them. It is thus a rhetorical handbook of ready-made counsels for a catalogue of joys and sorrows—Petrarch's *De inventione*, a layman's *summa confessorum*. Petrarch's own model was Seneca and his asserted vocation of directing souls toward inward freedom. It is embedded in Augustine's psychology and theology; it finds exemplification in Gregory the Great's *Book of Pastoral Care* and the whole medieval tradition of discipline and consolation, to borrow Thomas Tentler's phrase.

Yet Petrarch reasserts this ancient and Christian ideal in the context of lay culture rather than through the sacrament of penance. Through reading, the individual can detach himself from his miseries or prudently temper his joys and find the center of his self. However much the pursuit of more specifically secular goals such as wealth, prestige, power, and political effectiveness seems to characterize human behavior in the late Middle Ages and the Renaissance, the ideal of individual transcendence and internalization was an important element of Renaissance culture. Whether or not it is attached to belief in a relationship to divinity in one of its many forms (which it emphatically was in Petrarch's conception), this same ideal of psychically autonomous individuality has remained basic to Western culture. Petrarch's great contribution to the formation of the moral and cultural consciousness of the Renaissance was to project *this* vision of autonomy and alienation in terms comprehensible to his age. Its wide appeal was the reason for the popularity of his work. It was by virtue of his projection of the ideal of autonomy that he was entitled to call himself a philosopher, for, as was argued in chapter 1, it represents a poetic distillation of his reading of ancient philosophy. Finally, in confronting the excessive responses to the common human experiences of proud joy and despairing sorrow with the cool wisdom of reason, Petrarch dramatizes the new double consciousness of alienation and autonomy.

Alienation itself has become double and is manifested in the alternative modes of withdrawal from the common life of the world—arrogance and despair. Autonomy consists in "Reason's" reminders of the universal "misery of the human condition" and of the coexisting "dignity of man." In his summary chapter on "Happiness" in book 1 of *De remediis*, Petrarch points to the fragility of the happiness of even the truly virtuous man. The man who thinks himself happy when he is not is worst-off. "Truly they that govern themselves according to virtue, whom men account to be happy, and whom I also confess come nearest to felicity, endure continually most cruel conflicts of temptations within themselves, lying always open to many, grievous perils, and are never in security before their death; whether they know it or not, they are all to be reputed as wretched."[16]

Corresponding to this chapter is the one in book 2 on man's "sadness and misery." Setting forth his conception of the dignity that man received through his creation and the Incarnation, he says,

> You seek for reasons to make yourself sad on purpose when you ought rather to strive for the contrary so that you might rejoice in honorable gladness. But I know your practice. You are very diligent to procure your own harm. As to the baseness of your birth and the deformity of your body, whatever may be heaped up concerning your misery on those grounds by anyone's intellect or invention will be removed by the the general resurrection and will be wiped out by the worthiness of the glorification of your body, but it is

16. *De rem.*, 1.108; *Op. om.*, 110.

also diminished by the present beauty and the singular
majesty with which God has endowed man above all
the works of His hands. For how can baseness of birth
disparage the dignity of man?[17]

Petrarch was consciously replying to Innocent III's lucu-
brations on the vileness of the body, so that this treatise
on the dignity of man does belong at this point in his
scheme even though, as he argues following Augustine,
man's dignity rests in the trinitarian powers of his soul,
which was created in God's image. There is no difficulty in
confronting these two passages, for Petrarch as a good
rhetorician consoles according to circumstances and
disciplines according to necessity, delivering praise or
blame. These two opposing chapters were meant to sub-
sume the entire range of mankind's circumstantial elation
and humiliation.

In the extensive chapter on sundry griefs and pains
(book 2, chap. 114), Petrarch defends his use of rhetoric
and philosophy as a remedy for suffering, and the chapter
is in the form of a debate over the effectiveness of words.
Sorrow complains, "Alas, how tormented I am, poor
wretch, while you dispute and only offer philosophical
fables." Reason answers, "You are a wretch, if only because you call the rules of life fables." And Sorrow,
"These things are plausible in the schools and famous in
books, but they cannot enter into the wrack, or climb up
to the sickbed; they are more easily spoken and written
than practiced."[18] Reason concedes that they cannot work
for all but must sink into men's minds and be believed.
Virtue does not come to the suffering man by chance but
by deliberation, choice, and study. Admonitions can be a
cure of the mind, certainly, but also of the pains of the

17. *De rem.*, 2.93; *Op. om.*, 212.
18. *De rem.*, 2.114; *Op. om.*, 226.

body if the mind triumphs over them. "Pain is a bitter thing, cruel, horrible, sour, sharp, contrary to nature, odious to the senses, but notwithstanding, it can be made sweet by the assistance of virtue . . . and the greater vehemence of it can be made to feel more tolerable or not be felt at all." Sorrow asks, in the case of leprosy, "What good will your talk do for me?" Reason avers, "Truly very much, if you do not reject it, for it will discover you unto yourself, who seeing all things, sees not yourself."[19] This phrase epitomizes the heart of Petrarch's message.

At the same time that Petrarch began his *Remedies*, about 1355, Giovanni Boccaccio began his work on fortune, *On the Accidents of Famous Men*. In the last twenty years of his life, Boccaccio was to become a vigorous promoter of Petrarchan humanism and was himself the author of important humanist works, especially the favorite handbook of mythology of the Renaissance, the *De genealogia deorum gentilium*.[20] It is his earlier, more medieval work of 1349–51, *Il Decamerone*, however, for which he is universally remembered, rather than his charming, youthful classicizing romances and the humanistic Latin treatises of his mature years. The *Decameron* can of course be thought of as an *Umana Commedia* if it is forgotten that Dante called his poem simply *Commedia* because it ended felicitously before the throne of God. In a certain sense, however, the *Decameron* matches the structure of the *Commedia*. While the latter offers an imaginative journey through the parts of the other world that correspond to modes of earthly living, Boccaccio depicts three modes of earthly existence that can be said to correspond to the *Inferno, Paradiso,* and

19. *De rem.*, 2.114; *Op. om.*, 227–28.
20. Cf. Vittore Branca, *Boccaccio, the Man and His Works*, book 1, chap. 5, "Missions of Civil Diplomacy and Works of Humanistic Erudition (1352–60)," especially 108–10 and n. 31.

Purgatorio. They do not occur sequentially but are imagined to coexist simultaneously with each other. He begins his introductory "Preface to the Ladies" in which he depicts the horrors of the Black Death with an indication of its place in his narrative: "Let this gruesome beginning be like a steep and jagged mountain which wayfarers must surmount before they reach the pleasant delightful plain beyond. Then the greater the difficulty of the climb and descent, the keener the pleasure in the end; for as the extreme of happiness is never without its pain, so is suffering ended by supervening joy."[21]

Thus the total physical, social, and moral decay of the pestilence and the swinelike behavior it induced in the population is succeeded by the gathering in Santa Maria Novella of seven young Florentine ladies and three young men and their ascent of one of the many hills surrounding the city to escape the plague. Contrary to his simile, the plague occurred in the city of the plain, Florence, and the escape to joy involved an ascent. Both the hell of the disease-ridden city and the heaven of the villa and its gardens were actual, and Boccaccio hardly needed to exaggerate. But paradoxically these two poles of misery and joy, actual though they may have been, are offered by Boccaccio as fantasies concerning the extremes of earthly existence. Between them rests the actuality of everyday existence with its chances, temptations, sins, virtue, petty triumphs, and defeats described in the one hundred tales told in ten daily gatherings by each of the company of ten. But these are offered as fictional, and they have a definite 'traditional and even formulary provenance. Here then is Boccaccio's *Purgatorio.* Actuality is stranger than fiction, and fiction more actual than description.

The tales themselves contain other paradoxes. They

21. Singleton, 1:10; Winwar, xxiii.

cannot be reduced to a simple formula, for there is an amazing range of human types contained in them, from the utterly naive fool who is constantly abused to the shrewd operator who never misses an opportunity to do someone in, from the innocent to the sophisticate, from the astute scoundrel to the impossibly virtuous saint. Boccaccio frames the tales between these last two types, day one dealing with deceit and hypocrisy, day ten concerning itself with generosity and magnificence in love and other fields. The first and last tales, particularly, offer his notion of the extremes of good and evil in human character: Ser Ciappelletto, the evil notary from Prato, who deceived the good Franciscans of Burgundy into believing him to be a saint, who is called "perhaps the worst man ever born";[22] and Patient Griselda, who submitted passively to the worst humiliations a nobleman could devise against the poor country girl he had made his wife, and who was then restored to honor. The feeling of tension and ambiguity aroused by both these tales is patent, and they were quickly favorites among contemporary readers. Ser Ciappelletto turns out to be admirable in the unbelievable cleverness and fortitude with which he carries off his deception of the credulous and superstitious friars, just as Griselda seems weird and unbelievable in her patience. But both tales were meant to illustrate the strangeness of God's ways in creating his saints. Ciappelletto, the false saint, who was the worst man who ever lived, was innocently worshipped by his deceived admirers, and God accepted their prayers. Griselda the real saint seemed equally unlikely to become one, but the "divine spirits may sometimes descend from heaven, even to wretched hovels, just as in kingly palaces others may be born who are fitter to keep swine than to

22. Singleton, 1:29; Winwar, 3.

rule over men."[23] "But," as is said in the Ciappelletto story, "we must not flatter ourselves that this grace descends upon us through any merit of our own, for it is motivated by His goodness."[24]

Again Boccaccio most beautifully surrounds the core of his book with further margins of impossibility, yet makes these two "saints" in their unbelievability the necessary objects of a religious faith that can comfortably exist alongside of what we would be tempted to call his pictures of the "real world" of human sensuality, passion, and calculating intelligence, which must face the contingencies of other men's greed and of *fortuna*. What Boccaccio described as "all worldly things," which "are transient and mortal" and "are also replete with pain and toil within and without and subject to those infinite dangers which both enmesh and form part of our being," can receive a treatment that regards them as subject to autonomous elements in seeming separation and detachment from divine providence. God in his infinite distance from mankind may seem remote and unknowable and bound in an absolute state from which human affairs must seem insignificant and trivial, and it is necessary to trust that, as he has promised, providence rules and his grace is ever near.

Meanwhile it is necessary to confront things here as they are in their infinite contingency. Boccaccio exposes the threefold combination of elements that to his mind account for the play of events: man's sensual and passionate nature, which drives him into his myriad adventures and which he cannot overcome except with divine aid; the infinite yet contingent conjunctions of these individual courses of human action, which add up to

23. Singleton, 2:318; Winwar, 658–59.
24. For this and the quotations at the beginning of the next paragraph, see Singleton, 1:27–28; Winwar, 1–2.

fortune; and the prudential intelligence possessed by some men, which enables them to some extent to manipulate the two first elements to their own immediate advantage. Thus Boccaccio organizes the tales of the intervening eight days, between the total villainy of the pseudosaint and the immaculate purity of the unreal saint, around a series of combinations of these elements. The second day presents stories of those who, tormented by fortune, arrive at a happy outcome. In this, as in the rest, the happy outcome is also the consequence of pure chance and rarely due to any merit or astuteness on the part of the individual. The third day shows his characters succeeding in getting something they wanted through their own efforts, which also can happen, and getting back something they have lost; the fourth day sees a series of love affairs with disastrous endings, whereas the fifth sees happiness restored to lovers after accidents. Days six, seven and eight focus on human shrewdness and ingenuity (*astuzia, ingegno*) in getting out of unhappy situations, of wives in tricking their husbands and of tricks played on men or women. The categories are not that distinct; the three elements of natural passion, chance, and stupidity or astuteness tend to figure in all. Yet there is some effort to organize the tales into groups and to maintain the projected variation.

Boccaccio also presents a panoramic cross-section of medieval and Renaissance society, as well as of the geographic regions of Christian Europe and of the Moslem Mediterranean lands, with the Jews everywhere. This encyclopedic variety is sustained by means of the literary traditions on which he draws. But far more accentuated than all of these cultural, social, status, and religious differences is the common humanity of all individuals. Success and tragedy occur to individuals regardless of country, rank, wealth, moral condition, or intelligence.

Some are smarter than others, some are greedier, some are more lustful, but also some are nobler in an ethical sense. That true nobility comes from virtue and not from family or wealth is a litany of the later Middle Ages and the Renaissance from Dante's *Convivio* forward, and Boccaccio in his stories illustrates it. Alienation is universal and cannot be completely overcome, as all are subject to human frailty and knavery, either their own or others'. But some can behave with greater dignity and good sense. The passions of nature are there and cannot be eliminated. Some, however, can put them in their place, and occasionally when they do so an equally innate moral sense is aroused in their tormentors. It is this dignity that Boccaccio truly admires. As far as salvation is concerned no human rules apply, because it is God's grace that will determine that. A man can, by hypocrisy and trickery, induce others to believe he is a saint, and God will not refuse the good motives of those who worship a devil in the guise of a saint. Their prayers will be valid. The religious and the clergy are no better or worse than other men and can be as lustful or noble as any. The external goods of this life do not count for much even though most men strive for them. The capacity to maintain at least a belief in goodness in the midst of one's own and everyone else's inevitable moral failures is alone important.

Thus Boccaccio, like his friend Petrarch, even in what has been considered his most "medieval" work, visualizes the human world in terms of alienation and personal autonomy.[25] Also, like Petrarch, he sees this human world

25. I should like to pay my respects to Vittore Branca's famous conception of "Boccaccio Medievale," both in his book by that name and in his more recent comments in *Boccaccio, the Man and His Works*, book 2, chapter 1, "The Medieval Tradition." My conception of the moral and literary structure of *Il Decamerone* differs from but is not inharmonious with that of Branca. Perhaps

as divinely created and managed by a hidden providence that is inaccessible to man. Man can approach the divine best through striving to be most truly human, through what came to be called *humanitas* by humanists reviving the ideal of Cicero and Seneca and even of Lucretius. Petrarch's *Ratio* seemed to mean the pursuit of self-discovery and integrity more than pure moral discipline, and Boccaccio's man of *ingegno* and *astuzia* was not necessarily motivated by divinely inspired goodness. But within the limited powers of these qualities, framed by providence and divinity, men might still lead, even here, a more worthy life.

In Petrarch's and Boccaccio's moral philosophies divine purpose and human motivations could function side by side, and they could be reconciled as men of many sorts moved by their own powers toward a more self-consciously moral and noble existence. Theirs, which we hold to be a critical part of a "Renaissance" mode of consciousness, was not the only fourteenth-century solution to this problem, and it also was not inconsistent with some that came from more ecclesiastical and scholastic environments. But Petrarch's and Boccaccio's poetic response to the classical and Christian thought of antiquity yielded an outlook that closely corresponded to the experience of the literate middle class, not in the Italian cities alone, but also in those northern societies that so eagerly translated and assimilated their works.

While we may well think of the contribution of Petrarch,

---

the dichotomies *volgare*/classical and medieval/humanistic seem a little less sharp to me than to a literary historian in whose field these controversies continue to rage. Dante's *Commedia* I would also regard as thoroughly medieval in structure and style but as containing elements on which continuity with the succeeding humanistic culture could be established. So it is with Boccaccio, who even in his most "medieval" work presents a Renaissance vision of morality.

Boccaccio, and the other humanists to the culture of the Renaissance as primarily literary, historical, and moral, we are obscuring by those adjectives the deeply philosophical and theological character of this culture. Petrarch led the way toward the transformation of the insights of even contemporary scholastic thinkers into the kinds of thought patterns that could find direct application in the self-conception and life of the generally educated man. He did this by discovering the key to a similar transformation that had taken place in the ancient world among both pagan and Christian thinkers. There, too, especially in the world of Latin culture, philosophy was transformed into the *magistra vitae*, thus transcending the strictness and formalism of the old Academy and the Peripatetics. Moral philosophy, concerned with affecting the will toward the attainment of goodness, was nonetheless genuine philosophy, though its premises may well have been Protagorean and rhetorical. Such also were the ingredients of Renaissance humanism, which under Petrarch's formation and tutelage vindicated the importance of poetry and rhetoric as effectors of an intimate bond between reason and emotion, thought and action, intellect and will. Petrarchan humanism became a historical force mobilizing thought and letters against the blind impulsiveness of an illusory popular culture and the elitism of the philosophical schools.

List of Works Cited

(Abbreviations and short titles used in notes are given in parentheses.)

FRANCESCO PETRARCA TEXTS CITED

Opera omnia. Basel, 1554. (*Op. om.*)

Francesco Petrarca Prose. Edited by G. Martellotti and P. G. Ricci with E. Carrarra and E. Bianchi. Milan and Naples, 1955. (*Prose*)

Africa. Edited by Nicola Festa. Florence, 1926. (*Africa*)

Bucolicum Carmen. Translated and annotated by Thomas G. Bergin. New Haven and London, 1974. (*Carmen Bucolicum*)

Le familiari (*Familiarum rerum libri*). Edited by V. Rossi (vols. 1–3) and U. Bosco (vol. 4). Florence, 1933–1942. (*Rer. fam.*)

De otio religioso. Edited by Giuseppe Rotondi; completed by G. Martellotti. Studi e testi, 195. Vatican City, 1958. (*De otio*)

De remediis utriusque fortunae. In *Op. om.*, 1–256 (*De rem.*) English translation by Thomas Twyne, *Physike against Fortune, as well prosperous as adverse, conteyned in two Bookes.* London, 1559. (Twyne)

De sui ipsius et multorum ignorantia liber. Edited by L. M. Capelli. Paris, 1906; edited by P. G. Ricci in *Prose*, 710–67. (*De ignor.*) English translation (*On His Own Ignorance*) by Hans Nachod in *The Renaissance Philosophy of Man.* Edited by E. Cassirer, P. O. Kristeller, and J. H. Randall, Jr., 49–133. Chicago, 1948. (*De ignor.*, Nachod)

De viris illustribus. Edited by G. Martellotti, vol. 1. Florence, 1964.

De vita solitaria. In *Prose*, 285–581. (*De vit. sol.*) English translation by Jacob Zeitlin, *The Life of Solitude.* Urbana, Ill., 1924. (Zeitlin)

Invective contra medicum. Edited by P. G. Ricci. Rome, 1950. (*Contra. med.*)

Rerum memorandarum libri. Edited by Giuseppe Billanovich. Florence, 1945 (*Rer. mem.*)

Secretum (*De secreto conflictu mearum curarum*) *libri tres.* In *Prose*,

21-215. (*Secr.*) English translation by William H. Draper, *Petrarch's Secret, or The Soul's Conflict with Passion: Three Dialogues between Himself and S. Augustine*. London, 1911. (Draper)

OTHER TEXTS CITED

(Editions will be given only where used.)

Aristotle. *Ethica Nicomachea*. (*Eth. Nic.*)

———. *Metaphysica*. (*Metaph.*)

Saint Augustine. *Confessions*. Edited by Martinus Skutella. Stuttgart, 1969. (*Confess.*) English translation by J. G. Pilkington in *Basic Writings of Saint Augustine*, edited by W. J. Oates, 1:3–256. New York, 1948.

———. *De civitate Dei libri XXII.*

———. *De doctrina Christiana*. (*De doct. Christ.*)

———. *De magistro*. In *Corpus Christianorum, Series Latina* vol. 29. Edited by Klaus-Detlef Daur. Tournholt, 1970. English translation by G. C. Leckie in *Basic Writings of Saint Augustine*, edited by W. J. Oates, 1:361–95. New York, 1948.

Giovanni Boccaccio. *Opere di Giovanni Boccaccio*, vol. 6, *Il Decamerone*. Edited by Charles S. Singleton. Bari, 1955 (Singleton) English translation by Frances Winwar, *The Decameron of Giovanni Boccaccio*. New York, 1955. (Winwar)

Boethius. *De consolatione philosophiae*.

Cicero. *De divinatione*. (*De div.*)

———. *De inventione*. (*De inv.*)

———. *De senectute*. (*De sen.*)

———. *Hortensius*.

———. *Tusculanarum disputationum libri quinque*. Edited by T. W. Dougan and R. M. Henry. Cambridge, 1934. (*Tusc.*)

Justinus. *Epitome*.

Plato. *Phaedrus, Protagoras, Republic, Theaetetus*. In *The Dialogues of Plato*. Translated by B. Jowett. Reprint of 3d Oxford edition. New York, 1937.

Seneca. *De tranquilitate animae*.

———. *Epistulae ad Lucilium*. (*Epist.*)

Valerius Maximus. *Factorum ac dictorum memorabilium libri*. (*Fact. dict.*)

STUDIES

Hans Baron. "The Evolution of Petrarch's Thought: Reflections on the State of Petrarch Studies." *Bibliothèque d'Humanisme et Renaissance* 24 (1962): 7–41. Reprinted in Baron, *From Petrarch to Leonardo Bruni*, 7–50. Chicago, 1968. ("The Evolution of Petrarch's Thought")

——. "Petrarch: His Inner Struggles and the Humanistic Discovery of Man's Nature." In *Florilegium Historiale: Essays Presented to Wallace K. Ferguson*, edited by J. G. Rowe and W. H. Stockdale, 19–51. Toronto, 1971. ("Petrarch: His Inner Struggles")

——. "Petrarch's Secretum: Was It Revised—and Why?" *Bibliothèque d'Humanisme et Renaissance* 25 (1963): 489–530. Reprinted in *From Petrarch to Leonardo Bruni*, 51–101. ("Petrarch's Secretum")

Aldo S. Bernardo. *Petrarch, Scipio and the "Africa": The Birth of Humanism's Dream.* Baltimore, 1962. (*Petrarch and the "Africa"*)

Giuseppe Billanovich, "Petrarca e Cicerone," In *Miscellanea Giovanni Mercati*, vol. 4, 1–19. (Studi e Testi, 124). Vatican City, 1946

——. *Petrarca letterato*, vol. 1: *Lo scrittoio del Petrarca.* Rome, 1947.

——. "Petrarch and the Textual Tradition of Livy," *Journal of the Warburg and Courtauld Institutes* 14 (1951): 137–208.

Aurelia Bobbio. *Seneca e la formazione spirituale e culturale del Petrarca.* Florence, 1941.

Philotheus Boehner. Introduction to his edition of William of Ockham, *Tractatus de praedestinatione et de praescientia Dei et de futuris contingentibus.* St. Bonaventure, 1945. (Ockham, *Tractatus de praedestinatione*)

Umberto Bosco. "Il Petrarca e l'umanesimo filologico (postille al Nolhac e al Sabbadini)." *Giornale storico della letteratura italiana* 120 (1943): 65–119.

——. *Petrarca.* Turin, 1946.

William J. Bouwsma. "The Two Faces of Humanism: Stoicism and Augustinianism in Renaissance Thought." In *Itinerarium Italicum*, edited by H. A. Oberman with T. A. Brady, Jr., 3–60. Leiden, 1975. ("The Two Faces")

Vittore Branca. *Boccaccio Medievale.* Revised edition. Florence, 1970.

———. *Boccaccio, the Man and His Works.* New York, 1976.

Jacob Burckhardt. *The Civilization of the Renaissance in Italy.* New York, 1958.

Cambridge History of Later Greek and Early Medieval Philosophy. Edited by A. H. Armstrong. Cambridge, 1970.

William J. Courtenay. "Nominalism and Late Medieval Religion." In *The Pursuit of Holiness in Late Medieval and Renaissance Religion*, edited by C. Trinkaus with H. A. Oberman, 26–59. Leiden, 1974. ("Nominalism")

F. Edward Cranz. "Cusanus, Luther and the Mystical Tradition." In *The Pursuit of Holiness in Late Medieval and Renaissance Religion,* edited by C. Trinkaus with H. A. Oberman, 93–102. Leiden, 1974. ("Cusanus")

———. "1100 A.D.: Crisis for Us?" In *De Litteris, Occasional Papers in the Humanities*, 84–107. New London, 1978. ("1100 A.D.")

Angelo Crescini. *Le origini del metodo analitico—Il Cinquecento.* Udine, 1965. (*Le origini*)

E. R. Curtius. *European Literature and the Latin Middle Ages.* Translated by W. R. Trask. New York, 1953. (*European Literature*)

John Dillon. *The Middle Platonists, 80 B.C. to A.D. 220.* Ithaca, 1977.

Richard Douglas. "Talent and Vocation in Humanist and Protestant Thought." In *Action and Conviction in Early Modern Europe*, edited by T. K. Raab and J. E. Seigel, 261–98. Princeton, 1969. ("Talent and Vocation")

W. Fiske. *Francis Petrarch's Treatise "De remediis utriusque fortunae," Texts and Versions.* Bibliographical Notices, 3. Florence, 1888. (*Petrarch's Treatise "De remediis"*)

Neal W. Gilbert. "Richard de Bury and the 'Quires of Yesterday's Sophisms,'" In *Philosophy and Humanism, Renaissance Essays in Honor of Paul Oskar Kristeller.* edited by E. P. Mahoney, 229–57. Leiden, 1976. ("Richard de Bury and 'Sophisms'")

Thomas M. Greene. "The Flexibility of the Self in Renaissance Literature," In *The Discipline of Criticism, Essays in Literary Theory,*

Interpretation and History, edited by P. Demetz, T. Greene, and L. Nelson, Jr., 241-64. New Haven, 1968. ("The Flexibility of the Self")

————. "Petrarch and the Humanist Hermeneutic." In *Italian Literature, Roots and Branches: Essays in Honor of Thomas Goddard Bergin*, edited by G. Rimanelli and K. J. Atchity, 201-24. New Haven, 1976.

W. K. C. Guthrie. *A History of Greek Philosophy*, vol. 3, *The Fifth-Century Enlightenment*. Cambridge, 1969. (*Greek Philosophy* 3)

Klaus Heitmann. "Augustins Lehre in Petrarcas *Secretum*." *Bibliothèque d'Humanisme et Renaissance* 22 (1960): 34-53. ("Augustins Lehre")

————. *Fortuna und Virtus, Eine Studie zu Petrarcas Lebensweisheit.* Köln and Graz, 1957. (*Fortuna und Virtus*)

————. "L'insegnamento agostiniano nel *Secretum* del Petrarca." In *Atti del Terzo Congresso dell'Associazione Internazionale per gli Studi di Lingua e Letteratura Italiana: Petrarca e il Petrarchismo*, 187-93. Bologna, 1961. ("L'Insegnamento agostiniano")

Werner Jaeger. *Paideia: The Ideals of Greek Culture*, vol. 1. Translated by Gilbert Highet. New York, 1965. (*Paideia*)

Paul Oskar Kristeller. "Augustine and the Early Renaissance." In *Studies*, 355-72.

————. "Humanism and Scholasticism in the Italian Renaissance." In *Studies*, 553-83; also in *Renaissance Thought, the Classic, Scholastic, and Humanist Strains*, 92-119. New York, 1961.

————. "Il Petrarca, l'umanesimo e la scholastica a Venezia." In *La civiltà veneziana del Trecento*, 149-78. Venice, 1956.

————. "The Role of Religion in Renaissance Humanism and Platonism." In *The Pursuit of Holiness in Late Medieval and Renaissance Religion*, edited by C. Trinkaus with H. A. Oberman, 367-70. Leiden, 1974.

————. *Studies in Renaissance Thought and Letters*. Rome, 1956. (*Studies*)

Nicholas Mann. "The Manuscripts of Petrarch's *De remediis*, a Checklist." *Italia medioevale e umanistica* 14 (1971): 57-90.

Ugo Mariani. *Il Petrarca e gli Agostiniani.* Rome, 1959.

L. Minio-Paluello. "Il Fedone latino con note autografe del Petrarca."

Rendiconti dell'Accademia dei Lincei (Classe scienze morale) 8, no. 4 (1949): 107–13. ("Il Fedone latino")

Ruth Mohl. *The Three Estates in Medieval and Renaissance Literature.* New York, 1933; reprinted 1962.

Theodor E. Mommsen. "Petrarch's Conception of the 'Dark Ages,'" In *Medieval and Renaissance Studies*, edited by Eugene F. Rice, Jr., 106–29. Ithaca, 1959.

Rodolfo Mondolfo. *La comprensione del soggetto umano nell'antichità classica.* Florence, 1958, 1967; translation of original Spanish edition, Buenos Aires, 1955. (*La comprensione del soggetto*)

Ernest A. Moody. *Studies in Medieval Philosophy, Science and Logic: Collected Papers 1939–1969.* Berkeley and Los Angeles, 1975.

Pierre de Nolhac. *Petrarque et l'Humanisme*, 2 vols., 2d ed. Paris, 1907.

Heiko A. Oberman. "Fourteenth-Century Religious Thought: A Premature Profile." *Speculum* 53 (1978): 80–93. ("Fourteenth-Century Religious Thought")

———. *The Harvest of Medieval Theology.* Cambridge, Mass., 1963. (*Harvest*)

———. coeditor. *The Pursuit of Holiness in Late Medieval and Renaissance Religion.* Leiden, 1974. (*Pursuit of Holiness*)

———. "The Shape of Late Medieval Thought: The Birthpangs of the Modern Era." In *Pursuit of Holiness*, 3–25.

———. "Some Notes on the Theology of Nominalism with Attention to Its Relation to the Renaissance." *Harvard Theological Review* 53 (1960): 47–76. ("Notes on the Theology of Nominalism")

———. *Werden und Wertung, Vom Wegestreit zum Glaubenskampf.* Tübingen, 1977. (*Werden und Wertung*)

Heiko A. Oberman and Thomas A. Brady, Jr., editors. *Itinerarium Italicum: The Profile of the Italian Renaissance in the Mirror of Its European Transformations.* Leiden, 1975. (*Itinerarium*)

Erwin Panofsky. *Renaissance and Renascences in Western Art.* Stockholm, 1960; reprinted New York, 1969. (*Renaissance and Renascences*)

Elizabeth Pellegrin. *La bibliothèque des Visconti et des Sforza ducs de Milan au Xv^e siècle.* Paris, 1955.

R. R. Post. *The Modern Devotion: Confrontation with Reformation and Humanism.* Leiden, 1968. (*The Modern Devotion*)

Francisco Rico. *Vida u obra de Petrarca 1, Lectura del "Secretum."* Padua, 1974. (*Vida*)

———. "Precisazioni di cronologia Petrarchesca: Le 'Familiares' VIII ii–v, e i rifacimenti del 'Secretum'." *Giornale storico della letteratura italiana* 155 (1978): 481–525. ("Precisazioni")

Vittorio Rossi. *Studi sul Petrarca e sul Rinascimento.* Florence, 1930. (*Studi*)

Remigio Sabbadini. *Le scoperte dei codici latini e greci ne' secoli XIV e XV.* Florence, 1914; revised edition, edited by Eugenio Garin, Florence, 1967. (*Le scoperte*)

Jerrold E. Seigel. *Rhetoric and Philosophy in Renaissance Humanism.* Princeton, 1968. (*Rhetoric and Philosophy*)

Beryl Smalley. *English Friars and Antiquity in the Early Fourteenth Century.* Oxford, 1960. (*English Friars*)

Susan Snyder. "The Left Hand of God: Despair in Medieval and Renaissance Tradition." *Studies in the Renaissance* 12 (1965): 18–59. ("The Left Hand of God")

Leo Spitzer. "The Problem of Latin Renaissance Poetry." *Studies in the Renaissance* 2 (1955): 118–38. ("Latin Renaissance Poetry")

Francesco Tateo. *Dialogo interiore e polemica ideologica nel "Secretum."* Florence, 1965. (*Dialogo interiore*)

Thomas N. Tentler. *Sin and Confession on the Eve of the Reformation.* Princeton, 1977. (*Sin and Confession*)

Charles Trinkaus. *In Our Image and Likeness: Humanity and Divinity in Italian Humanist Thought*, 2 vols. London and Chicago, 1970. (*Image*)

———. "Protagoras in the Renaissance: An Exploration." In *Philosophy and Humanism: Renaissance Essays in Honor of Paul Oskar Kristeller*, edited by E. P. Mahoney, 190–213. Leiden, 1976. ("Protagoras in the Renaissance")

———. "The Religious Thought of the Italian Humanists and the Reformers: Anticipation or Autonomy?" In *Pursuit of Holiness*, 339–66. ("Italian Humanists and the Reformers")

Charles Trinkaus and H. A. Oberman, editors. *The Pursuit of Holi-*

ness in Late Medieval and Renaissance Religion. Leiden, 1974. (*Pursuit of Holiness*)

B. L. Ullman. *Studies in the Italian Renaissance.* Rome, 1955. (*Studies*)

Mario Untersteiner. *The Sophists.* Translated by Kathleen Freeman. Oxford, 1954.

Cesare Vasoli. *La dialettica e la retorica dell'Umanesimo: "Invenzione" e "Metodo" nella cultura del XV e XVI secolo.* Milan, 1968. (*Dialettica e retorica*)

Laszlo Versényi. *Socratic Humanism.* New Haven, 1963.

Roberto Weiss. *The Renaissance Discovery of Classical Antiquity.* Oxford, 1969. (*Renaissance Discovery*)

Siegfried Wenzel. *The Sin of Sloth: "Acedia" in Medieval Thought and Literature.* Chapel Hill, 1967. (*The Sin of Sloth*)

Ernest Hatch Wilkins. *Life of Petrarch.* Chicago, 1961.

———. *Petrarch's Correspondence.* Padua, 1960.

———. *Studies in the Life and Works of Petrarch.* Cambridge, Mass., 1955. (*Studies*)

Ronald Witt. "Coluccio Salutati and the Conception of the *Poeta Theologus* in the Fourteenth Century." *Renaissance Quarterly* 30 (1977): 538-63.

Index

("Petrarch" within entries will be abbreviated "P")

145